This book is dedicated to all my Nieces and Nephews

When Scared. Show Courage.

Through Adversity. Never, Ever Give-Up.

Alone and Lost. Take a Single Step.

Through Pain. Gain Strength.

If Knocked Down. Stand-Up.

Face Challenges with Sheer Determination.

Gain Wealth. By Sharing.

Attack Deceit with Ferocity.

Look Out and Not In.

See Ignorance and Educate.

Let Love. Fill Your Heart.

Stand Together when Called.

But Most of All,

      When Darkness Falls. Shine.

# Introduction

This is a personal thing, but I hate picking up books full of pages and pages of introduction. Discussing the style of the book, with really long words, thanking people you don't even know. So as a first time author, here's mine, short & simple and tells you want you need to know:

-- This is a USA travel guide which skims over the major cities, and thereby tells you about "real" America, not the America you repeatedly see on television or in the movies. As a personal biography it designed to be a light read.

-- If you live in America and are well travelled you may be put off by this book, but don't be. This book is something to flick through on your 4 hour lay-over if you're sick of reading your newspaper or magazine. It will hopefully make you chuckle and I'm sure you'll recognize some of the places and characters I mention.

-- The author is not a "snow-bird", but a European in her thirties, not afraid to try 'everything' and 'anything' !

-- As much as possible the proceeds of this book are going to charity (not made up ones, but real ones detailed on the website). So you should feel good buying it.

-- This book was a personal journey for the author after a series of well-documented and life changing events. She hopes you might find inspiration in it too.

# RULE No.1 :

I had to travel by following the letters of the alphabet in order. So A, B, C, D and so on.....even if that meant traveling thousands of miles in the opposite direction.

# RULE No.2 :

No major towns or cities. Although I was allowed to visit them, they could not count as a letter in the book. A major town or city was normally determined by if it had an international airport, cathedral, large population size (etc).

# RULE No.3 :

On my travels I would talk to ordinary Americans and ask them to recommend places to visit and Vote. People also voted on the website or via e-mail.

www.atozeeacrossamerica.com

We welcome any feedback regarding the book including grammatical or fact corrections. Don't be shy. atoz.acrossamerica@gmail.com

# *A* *is for......* Albuquerque

**Albuquerque, New Mexico -** With a surprisingly multicultural history and diversity, Albuquerque is a great long weekend destination year round. Sante Fe is a "must-do" stop off. Get's My Vote for : Best Art & Crafts Destination the USA.

On arriving in New Mexico, you'll see why the State is known as "The Land of Enchantment". Whether you're fishing in the Pecos Wilderness, hiking the Sandia Mountains, or lazily horseback riding through the fiery red landscapes of the Rio Grande. Your day will end beneath multi-coloured sunsets contrasting the blackness of the diamond twinkling night sky.

Although many States may claim to possess history, culture, art and a vacation lifestyle. Having travelled all 50, I am happy to announce that New Mexico delivers. With its long, sometimes turbulent, history and colourful mix of culture and peoples the state is truly unique.

Who would have thought it, a place named in a one hit wonder by Prefab Sprout back in the 1980's would offer so much to the traveling tourist. (Check out—You Tube—"The King of Rock and Roll").

And so it was by accident, I started the A to Zee Journey Across America with the letter "A" for Albuquerque. Little did I know at the time, once started I would travel over 80,000(+) miles and it would take over 3 years to complete.

USA – Southwest Region

Map data ©2011 Google, INEGI - Terms of Use

Albuquerque is a multicultural community represented by more than 70 different ethnicities some of which date back nearly twelve thousand years, stemming from Pueblo Indians, Hispanic and Western legacies.

So it is not surprising to find Albuquerque offers a varied mix of cultural museums, food and arts. As well as hundreds of unique tours, global events and performances throughout the year.

Check out this website for more information: www.itsatrip.org/culture.

# Albuquerque, New Mexico

One of my favourite places to visit was the National Atomic Museum. Soon to be named something more "politically correct" which is understandable if you do any reading about New Mexico's atomic history. If WWII is an interest, then research the Manhattan Project and I would highly recommend a visit to the fascinating city of Los Alamos.

Continuing the geeky-theme if you are a sci-fi fan and dream of meeting Little Green Men with Big Black Eyes then you'll love the UFO Festival held in July. Any event that recommends you pack "Tin foil, green body paint and a Ray gun" - I'm there!

For more recommendations like this check out this great book called : Party Across America by Matt Guerriero.

Also worth a visit (at least outside) is the National Hispanic Cultural Centre. For no other reason than to see the ugly shaped building, it looks like something from an 70's sci-fi series. Even Ernő Goldfinger (an infamous designer of concrete monstrosities) would have been proud of it. Honestly it makes the National Theatre in London look pretty!

One of the things that makes New Mexico so "enchanting" is its understated appeal. To prove this Albuquerque boasts THE World's Largest Hot Air Balloon Festival in October each year. As well as one of America's *only* Native America Pageants, when there is the Crowning of Miss Indian World. Aw' how enchanting is that...

But no trip to Albuquerque would be complete without undertaking a pre-booked Pueblo Village tour. Where you get shown around by one of the Pueblo Indian village inhabitants. One of the customs I found quite amusing was this one :

*"Do not refuse an invitation to eat.
Eat a little bit, even if you have already eaten and are not hungry.
Do not linger at the table after eating. Do not ask questions of your host."*

This reminded me alittle of Thanks Giving or Christmas when you arrive at the second or third house to eat, drink and say nice things. Despite the fact you are hung-over and just want to curl up in-front of a TV repeat.

Being in New Mexico there is of course the unrelenting craving to purchase something relating to chili's. My craving satisfied I left with a dried chili necklace (chile ristra) and that household essential Chili Fairy Lights!

Chili first came to New Mexico with Spanish settlers in 1598 and today more chili is grown here than in any other state. Trust me, you will eventually succumb to the chili"s power...

With this in mind, you might want to check out the Fiery Foods and BBQ Show which is held here every spring.

# Albuquerque, New Mexico

As the name suggests they sell crazy HOT chili sauce to entertain your family with on the 4th July after a few tequila's. My favorite being the bottle called One F**-ing Drop at a Time!

You will also be wooed by the Native American lure of Turquoise when visiting the must-see historic Old Town. Here you can shop, eat and enjoy some traditional music in the town plaza throughout the year.

I had "The Best" Huevos Rancheros in America at the Church Street Café for breakfast. Trust me I ate these a lot in California, Texas & Arizona. But the ones in Albuquerque were amazing.

It's also good to know that New Mexico actively runs projects to ensure the finest locally grown produce including wines, vegetables and meats are used in it's restaurant menus.

No trip to Albuquerque would be complete without a quick drive across to Santa Fe. Although it's reputation has been "Californianized" (thank goodness that is not a 'real' word)!

Santa Fe is officially the oldest established Capital City in the US. The impressive Adobe Palace of the Governors dates from 1610 and is the oldest public building in America. Originally housing Spanish officials, soldiers and their families.

But it is for The Arts, Santa Fe is now well known for and deservingly so.

It has been estimated 1 in 6 of their residents earns a living in an art related industry. Most people head to Canyon Road which opens late on Friday evenings, just in time for the San Francisco and Los Angeles flights to arrive!

But that is just a small selection of the 250 galleries and several premier arts events that take place each year. I counted at least 15 museums as well as 8 different performing arts center's including an opera venue with views that would rival Sydney.

But if you take the time and look hard enough you will find some little gems in Santa Fe. I found an Arts Fair outside the New Mexico Museum of Arts. Home to local struggling artists, who present their various works of art to passers-by without the intimidation of shop window prices.

# A *is for......*

# Albuquerque

I purchased 2 stencil prints from a local Hispanic artist called AnaMaria Samaniego. Who to my delight had *not* been 'Californian-ized' and was more than happy to talk about the techniques she had used. And the whereabouts of the two locations that featured in the stencils I purchased.

If you encounter such an opportunity I would strongly encourage you to take it. As I found Sante Fe was one of The Best Arts and Crafts destinations across the whole 50 States.

Having been married myself by Elvis at the famous White Wedding Chapel in Las Vegas, I was thrilled to find out that New Mexico has its very own town called Las Vegas. Plus it's just as easy to get hitched there.

First, get your shotgun! Sorry, your intended, $25 (in cash, of course) and a photo ID.

Take it to the County Clerk's office in Santa Fe for your license. There is no waiting period or other requirements.

Faster than you can say "What the hell happen last night!"

So Albuquerque was a great choice as my first destination. Chosen completely at random when I was stood at the departure desk at LAX one Friday after work.

Being 6 months as a new resident in Los Angeles and so fed-up of being alone on the weekend. Anywhere I thought, would be better than that. Albuquerque just happened to be the first destination on the departures list.

With its year-round climate it's perfect as a long weekend destination.

It wasn't until I visited some of the states like north eastern Pennsylvania and Massachusetts nearly 12 months later that I found such an interesting history to match New Mexico's.

Plus it's location near the famous 4 Corners, where the States Arizona, Colorado, Utah and New Mexico meet makes it an ideal spot for further travel.

I had a great time and like the Native American, Hispanic settlers and Frontier Scouts before me. I was hoping America would vote for me to visit New Mexico again.

VOTED FOR BY THE AUTHOR

**BEST IN AMERICA**

The Church Café, 2111 Church St NW

*Huevos Rancheros*

Albuquerque

# IF YOU HAVE MORE TIME ...

## Outdoors People

Trout is abundant in local rivers. The areas around Pecos, Jemez and Velarde Rivers are worth a visit and further research. For the boaters, Lakes at Abiquiu, Cochiti and McAlister are for you.

I went horseback riding in Pecos, lazily trekking through stunning woodlands for an afternoon. Amazing scenery, loved it.

If you would prefer to get onto the water then you can white water raft and kayak around the Embudo area. It is very popular because of it's narrow stretch of water in the Rio Grande gorge which makes the waters warm.

## History, Culture & Gifts

For the Arts Buff's this whole region is Georgia O'Keefe country. She loved to paint New Mexico with its red rock, sandstone cliff and juniper studded hills which run parallel to the Chama River. If you are a fan of her work then the adobe hacienda Ghost Ranch is a must see.

Looking for that unique gift, then head to the local pueblo at Embodo and Ohkay who have roadside stands selling fruits, seasonal foods and hand-made crafts. Also worth a visit is Jemez Springs which has a public soaking Victorian-era bathhouse where its name originates known as the "Place of the Boiling Waters'.

## Photographers (People & Places)

Suggested photography spots include the San Ildefonso Pueblo with its cottonwoods, rushing Rio Grande and Black Mesa all make for that perfect shot. Or head to Valle Grande outside Jemez, here you can see the huge three-million-year-old collapsed volcano crater. Or check out the monoliths at Kasha Katuwe in the Tent Rocks National Monument.

A must-see for photographers are the Nambe Falls, Comanche Point and Valle Vidal, all stunning waterfalls. Or head to the Sandia Mountains and Sandia Crest for breath-taking panoramic views of the whole area.

## Only in America.....

Go to Cerrillos with your buddies and dress-up as cowboys and play westerns! Yee, har!  Check out: www.newmexico.org/western/explore/cerrillos.php

Santuario de Chimayo (aka) Loudres of the Southwest draws pilgrims from around the world because of the healing powers of its "miraculous dirt" found in the 19th century Chapel.

Somewhat surprisingly the English novelist D.H Lawrence (of Lady Chatterley's Lover fame) had a fascination with New Mexico and choose Taos as his final resting place.

# USA VOTED - TOP 6 'OTHER' LETTER "A" DESTINATIONS ...

### Arlington Cemetery, Virginia
Washington Dulles International Airport is 28 miles or approx. 35mins.

### Acadia National Park, Maine
Bangor International Airport is 66 miles or approx. 1hrs 40mins.

### Asheville, North Carolina
Greenville-Spartanburg International Airport is 56 miles or 1hr 15mins.

### Acme, LA, MI, NC, PA, WA, WY
Pittsburgh Airport is 67 miles or approx. 1hr 30mins.

### Annapolis, Maryland
Baltimore/Washington International Airport is 17 miles or approx. 37mins.

### Alexandria, Virginia
Baltimore/Washington International Airport is 41 miles or approx. 55mins.

# $B$ _is for......_  $\mathbf{B}$end

**Bend, Oregon** - When combined with Portland is a great winter destination. Wrap-up warm, enjoy the micro-brews and everything this eclectic city has to offer. Then enjoy the breath taking scenery to Bend warming in a log fired cabin.

For the letter "B" America voted for places like The Badlands, South Dakota, Brooklyn, NYC and Branson, Missouri. But early on, the surprise winner was a little-known place called Bend in central Oregon.

Combined with a trip to Portland this is a great winter weekend get-away. To my surprise the best part about going to Bend was not necessarily Bend itself, but the actual journey getting there from Portland.

The contrasting scenery went from the downtown setting of Portland to the Three Sister's snow -capped mountains, vast green woodlands to humid yellow flat prairies. Of all the journeys I made on my eighty thousand plus miles this one offered the most variety in such a short space of time. Even better than some of the more famous routes like the Million Dollar Highway, Colorado, Route 66 or the Pacific Coast Highway in California.

You are faced with a matte pastel skyline equally layered with pinks, reds and turquoise set against the white snow and distant pale silver moon. Such a sight I thought, would have made Mark Rothko (once an Oregon native) magnanimous in appreciation.

When travelling to the State of Oregon, most people begin their journey at the State's biggest airport and city, the fantastically eclectic City of Portland.

Portland is called the City of Roses due to its famed international Rose Test Garden in Washington Park.

The garden which opened in 1917 was a safe haven for European hybrid roses in danger of being bombed during World War I.

In 1940 the garden became the first official test garden in America. Therefore allowing American's and the world the first glimpse of new rose varieties.

Portland was one of my favourite US cities to visit for a number of reasons.

## Bend, Oregon

One, was that it is made-up of individually distinct districts and neighbourhood's with names like Nob Hill, Belmont, Hawthorn Pearl and Hollywood.

Each district having an oasis of shops, restaurants, theatres and gardens.

VOTED FOR BY THE AUTHOR
BEST IN AMERICA
Fish & Chips & English Food
Portland Saturday Market
Portland

Secondly, what makes such a large city like Portland so likable, is the fact you can easily walk around the downtown areas on foot. This is unheard of for a major US city, as normally you are forced to drive everywhere.

So grab yourself a street map and see how many Simpson's characters you can spot when walking around. As Matt Groening is famously a native of Portland.

You will find names like Quimby Street, Flanders Street, Montgomery Park and the Burnside Bridge.

Having been to Munich, I was pleased to learn that Portland is affectionately known as the Munich on the Willamette.

Since an explosion of micro-brews and beers in the 80's. Portland now has 32 breweries more than any other City in the world. Yes, you heard me right, in the World!

Even better if you have any shoppers in your party, the Portland Saturday market is within walking distance of many of them. So they can shop whilst you drink, perfect!

The Saturday Market, ironically also open on Sundays, March through December.

Is the largest continuously operating open air market for handcrafted goods in the US.

I really enjoyed it, there is an excellent variety of weird and wonderful items for the home. Many stalls sold the micro-brews as well as cooking ingredients.

It you have ever spent any time in Pike's Place, Seattle, Terminal Market, Philly, Camden Market, London, Rocks Market Sydney, you'll know what I mean.

I headed to the Food Area at the entrance. Which offered a wide variety of hot and cold foods for any palette from all across the United States.

# B *is for......*

# B end

This was my first experience of kettle corn (pop corn) being made by hand in a large copper cylinder.

The lady behind the stall was kind enough to allow me to have a go at making it. I was rubbish!

To my delight I had the opportunity to be reminded of foods from my native England.

There was a market stall called Milke's Cafe serving Pies, Sausage Rolls and Cornish pasties.

Mike was a Scouser (from Liverpool) so I can vouch for them being authentic.

The homeless man I met later and shared them with, seemed to agree with my culinary opinion.

I also had fish and chips from a stall on the corner. They were fantastic, better than many I have had at home. I found out the secret recipe, which I promised I would not share. Needless to say his batter mix contained cornmeal!

Right next door they were selling the most famous local micro-brew called Rogue Beer.

Who would have thought it, a small piece of England in Portland!

Leaving Portland if you head towards the north west you get to scenic Columbia County.

With William Matte Valley wine country to the south. The Columbia River Gorge is to the east and the Pacific coast to the west.

This whole region is packed with many places to explore and plenty of things to do in the summer and through the snow season.

To get to Bend, I headed north east towards Mount Hood. Mount Hood is very impressive shattering the horizon with it's snow-topped peak.

It you get a chance to stop off here they have fantastic salmon fishing in the summer and wood burning log cabins to snuggle-up in-front of in the winter.

The repeating scenery of woodlands, snow capped mountains and vast plains was stunning.

If you are lucky enough to be in this area and have the time, stop off often and enjoy the variety of the scene. You are spoilt with dramatic landscape in all directions.

On arriving in Bend first glimpses are just alittle anti-climatic compared to the journey. But certainly worth a passing visit all the same.

Bend grew in the early 1800's when the early pioneers began homesteading the valleys. Making their fortune by selling food goods, minerals and the milling of lumber.

Originally called "Farewell Bend" by the lumber settlers in the early 1900's. Bend is central Oregon's largest city with over 2.5 million acres of national forest.

Surprisingly though, it only has around 77,000 residents.

Located on the eastern edge of the Cascade and Deschutes River it is engulfed by the Deschutes National Forest. It is because of this that Bend became populated by the pioneers as it was one of the few places you could cross the river.

# Bend, Oregon

Today many of the downtown restaurants remember their pioneering past by serving the huge Pioneer Breakfast. Consisting of corn bread, eggs, stew and potatoes.

Bend itself, at an elevation of over 3,000 feet is famed for its majestic snowcapped peaks. Like the Three Sisters, Broken Top Mountain and Mt. Jefferson as well as its high desert skyline.

So it doesn't get too hot in the summer but has plummeting temperatures in the winter making it a perfect ski-destination.

There are over 3,500 ski-slopes, 56km of cross-country ski trails and 560 miles of snow mobile tracks. Not forgetting for the less adventurous there is snow tubing, snow shoeing and dog sled rides.

Bend describes itself as a place "where the warmth of a mountain town embraces every visitor as its own". I would definitely agree with this.

I went in the autumn when the weather was beginning to turn, it was really nice to enjoy a warm fire, hot food and welcoming company in the evenings.

For anyone who enjoys quiet slopes and sedate après-ski this would be the perfect destination. Bend has some fantastic snow pursuits.

If you have more time not too far from away is McKenzie Pass. A winding, narrow two-lane road which the old wagon routes used to take.

It provides stunning views of the Three Sisters Mountains and Washington Mount.

For hikers head to the Belknap Crater here waterfalls emerge from the plummeting vertical drops. Or the 1-mile Proxy Falls Loop, this meandering trek through dense forest presents two spectacular waterfalls plunging over moss-covered cliffs.

I encountered hundreds of early pioneer towns on my A to Zee journey across America. But the journey through northern California into Oregon onto Portland then Bend was fantastic.

I would highly recommend it as the perfect wrap-up warm autumn or winter destination.

Driving around Oregon was a real treat with its variety of landscapes and changeable weather. In some respects it felt like driving around the Highlands of Scotland or the emerald Isle of Southern Ireland.

It left a lasting impression on me, one that stayed with me for the rest of my journey across the US.

# IF YOU HAVE MORE TIME ...

## Outdoors People

Kayakers and rafters shoot through the exciting triple waterfalls of the Deschutes River. The Deschutes, Metolius and Crooked Rivers are also popular with fly-fishers with 500 miles of streams and rivers stocked with trout and steelhead. Or try the area around Newberry Monument with its water filled volcanic craters offering a different landscape and excellent mountain lake fishing.

Golfers have over 20 top-rated courses close-by to Bend. There is a Jack Nicklaus Designed Course at The Club At Pronghorn which has fantastic views around the course.

A must-see for all dedicated climbers, 300miles east of Bend, is the 8,000 feet deep Hells Canyon. The deepest river gorge in North America.

## History, Culture & Gifts

There is the usual shopping in downtown Bend and the Old Mill District. After that I would recommend a scenic stroll around Drake Park's Mirror Pond. For something alittle bit different look out for the Central Oregon Saturday Market offering a wide variety of local arts and crafts at this unique outdoor market in downtown Bend.

Shopping in Portland, make sure you buy some of the micro-brews to take home as unique gifts.

Also check out Voodoo doughnuts open 24/7 a Portland institution is a must-taste for first-time visitors to Portland. After a few too many micro-brews these were perfect.

## Photographers (People & Places)

Look out for the Big Bend Annual Exhibition of Photography in January. Or enter the Fruit-Loop a 35 mile trail of orchards along Highway 35 with festivals and events all year.

Walk or a drive to the top of Pilot Butte for panoramic views of Bend and its volcanic peaks. At 511 ft high you can see high desert vistas as well as nine snow-capped Cascade Peaks. An even finer view can be found at the Newberry National Volcanic Monument stretching from Paulina Peak to the Deschutes River featuring lava formations and waterfalls.

But my favourite and a "must-see" was Crater Lake heading 2000ft high you get to a naturally made lake surrounded by ancient snow capped volcanos. It is on a Yellowstone, Yosemite level of awesome.

## Only in America.....

Oregon has more ghost towns than any other State in the US.

The Don Brown Rosary Collection in Oregon is the world's largest rosary collection.

Check out the unique floating dance floor at the Crystal Ballroom, it moves to the beat thanks to its ball bearing rocker arm.

Todd Roberts in the 1990s a maintenance crew worker in Portland decided to use his creative talents in the cities asphalt markings. He added hats and other amusing objects to the characters in the cycling lane. See how many you can spot in downtown Portland.

# USA VOTED - TOP 6 'OTHER' LETTER "B" DESTINATIONS ...

**Badlands & Black Hills, South Dakota**
Black Hills Airport is 128 miles, Rapid City Regional Airport is 31 miles or approx. 45mins.

**Brooklyn, New York**
LaGuardia Airport is 13 miles or approx. 30mins.

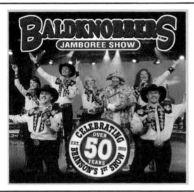

**Branson, Missouri**
Springfield National Airport is 55 miles or approx. 1hr 5mins.

**Bryce Canyon, Utah**
Bryce Canyon Airport 5.1 miles or Salt Lake City is 290 miles or approx. 5 hours.

**Bismarck, North Dakota**
Bismarck Municipal Airport is 4 miles or 10mins.

**Boulder, Colorado**
Boulder Municipal Airport is 4 miles or 15mins.

# *C* is for...... *C*oney Island

**Coney Island, New York -** Has a long and turbulent history which has proudly defined it. Whether you "Love it" or "Hate it" Coney Island will certainly leave a lasting impression and probably for all the wrong reasons!

"C" is for Coney island, New York City - There are so many adjectives one could use to describe Coney Island it is hard to know which to select. Words that spring to mind are brash, tacky, saucy and raw; which you may think have negative connotations, but you would you be wrong. This "naughty but nice" resort has a glittering past packing in hundreds of thousands of visitors each year trying to escape the heat of New York City.

Ironically it was these visitors who psychically created the Coney Island of today, once an isolated island, it only become connected to the mainland by landfill trash! Now it sits as a peninsula of southern Brooklyn, NY on the east coast of the Atlantic Ocean.

The original Coney Island in Ireland dated back to the 12th Century. But following European settlement to the USA in the early 16th century the English word Coney or Gaelic Coinín (their word for rabbit) is were its name originates. In the early 1800s the construction of elegant hotels and easier transportation links meant that Coney Island began attracting more and more holiday makers by the end of the century. Electricity had replaced the steam railroads and new attractions like a carousel and the infamous Coney Island Elephant arrived for the first time.

For many immigrants arriving in New York "Lucy" the Coney Island Elephant, was often their first glimpse at the Land of Opportunity and not the famed Ellis Island, Statue of Liberty.

## USA - Northeast Region

History has shown us, nothing lasts forever and after World War II the popularity of Coney Island began to contract.

Due to the convenience of automobiles, the closing of amusement parks and finally New York street gang problems signalled the end of an era.

Since then its history has been a sorry and sordid tale of battles between bureaucrats, developers, owners and its inhabitants. Today Coney Island is trying to reinvent itself. What into, is still open to debate!

# Coney Island, New York

To help you make your own mind up about whether you would "Love It" or "Hate It" here were my highlights :

Coney Island is considered the birthplace of the hot-dog because of Nathan Handwerker who started his hot dog career back in the 1920s. To attract crowds, he dressed ten freshly shaven homeless people as doctors. When the public saw his sign "If doctors eat our hot dogs, you know they're good!" He became so successful the police had to be called in to unblocked the broad sidewalk in front of his stand.

Today annually on the 4th July, Nathan's hot dog stand established in 1960 holds its annual hot dog eating contest. Over 40,000 people attend the event with an estimated 1.7m viewers watching it on ESPN. One of the most famous champions is Joey Chestnut who won after chowing down 54 hot dogs and buns in less than ten minutes.

My second highlight would be the newly opened amusement park called Scream Zone. It's a group of four scary rides; Sling-shot, which throws two people 150 feet in the air at 90 miles an hour. The tension before you are thrown being the worst bit !

The much tamer horse themed roller coaster called Steeplechase. Or the Soarin' Eagle ride when you are strapped into what feels like a giant sleeping bag and sent down a helter-skelter structure.

But for the ultimate thrill seekers you should try Xenobia.

Ever wondered what it might feel like jumping off a tall building? Then this tumbling, falling sensation at vast heights is definitely for you.

Then there is of course the world famous Coney Island Mermaid Parade. Which takes place on Surf Avenue (the best place to see it) and the Boardwalk at the start of summer. In the spirit of Mardi Gras, it features floats, mermaids and sea creatures of every shape and size. With an equally festive and colourful crowd. A highlight is the crowning of the Merman and Mermaid King and Queen at the Mermaid Parade Ball.

Expect lots of nudity and scantily clad costumes. Believe it or not it is legal in New York State for women to be topless in public as long as you are not doing business! So flaunt it. This being Coney Island, no-one will even notice anyway!

CI9 FIRST TIME EVER MERMAID PARADE 2009
oney Island Dancer

One surprising fact about Coney Island is hidden in its subway station called Coney Island–Stillwell Avenue. It is the largest elevated Metro station in North America. The entire station was rebuilt in 2001–05 modernizing it with a large solar-panel canopy covering all eight tracks. Its *the* largest renewable-energy mass transit station in the United States and has inspired many other projects around the world.

So when you arrive take the time to look-up at the roof and solar panelling. I found it a testament to Coney Island's die hard spirit. Thus proving it's not just all hot dogs and boardwalk antics!

# Coney Island, New York

But my absolute favourite thing was The Coney Island Dancers. What looks from afar like a random group of people having a "Boogie on the Boardwalk" is actually a well organized membership club. Of course, there are no rules, all shapes, sizes & colours are encouraged.

They describe themselves as "The Pulse of House & Disco Music". Check out:

www.coneyislanddancers.com/

The members tend to be regulars and obviously come dressed-up. Membership is considered a privilege and to join you have to provide your "dancing credentials".

I am proud to tell you I had the honour of becoming a Coney Island Dancer. Who would have thought it, all those endless nights dancing away in Ibiza were totting-up for a Coney Island Dancer loyalty/membership card!

Whatever you decide to do in Coney Island I would recommend washing the whole experience down with vast amounts of the Coney Island Beer and the archery clogging delights of the boardwalk. There were so many foods I had never seen before.

The highlight being Deep Fried Oreo's and a Funnel Cake, a huge stringy doughnut made into a nest covered in chocolate. As well as frankfurters and wieners of every kind, Gyros (kebab to me and you) sea-food, and don't forget Shish-Ke-Dad! Just looking at all the colourful eateries is an experience.

That night I went to see Burlesque Show On the Boardwalk. Ridiculously camp, it was fantastically over-the-top and not to be missed.

VOTED FOR BY THE AUTHOR
BEST IN AMERICA
Fried Food
The Boardwalk
Coney Island

I think it is this brash honesty of "It Is, What It Is..." that makes Coney Island so heart-warming.

Ok so some of the fare rides are rickety, but it's not trying to be Disneyland. The food is greasy, but no-one expects Michelin Stars. The raunchy burlesque side shows seduce fantasy and fetish, so don't expect to run on Broadway.

Coney Island is not the most picturesque place I went to in American, but it was certainly one of the most fun. Its "Naughty but Nice" charm is what makes it unique and definitely worth a visit.

"Love it" or "Hate it" it is proud of it's roots. I hope it continues to delight and entertain for a long time to come.

# IF YOU HAVE MORE TIME ...

## Outdoors People

The many sights of Coney Island are spread out so be prepared to walk a lot. The good news is that all the main attractions are no further than 3 blocks away from the Boardwalk. So if you keep going inwards away from the ocean and then back again down another street you can't really go wrong. Trust me you'll remember this advise at 4am after a few Coney Island beers!

If you start at the New York Aquarium, head towards the Pier and you will hit the amusement area. Heading in the same direction away from the pier you will hit Surf Avenue, Steeplechase Plaza and eventually Seaside Gateway.

This whole area surrounding the Boardwalk is about 3 to 6 blocks square and is full of things to look at and do.

## History, Culture & Gifts

Sideshows By The Seashore is the last permanently housed place in the USA where you can experience the thrill of a traditional ten-in-one circus sideshow.

Alternatively the Coney Island Girlie Freakshow at Burlesque at the Beach houses American's favourite game show This or That. Providing a kinky, exaggerated and bizarre night out. Hey, have fun, let your hair down and let the strange, comedic experience begin!

In recent years Coney island has seemed under threat, resulting in the development of Coney Island USA. A non-profit organization founded in the belief that:
"19th century American popular culture gave birth to a democratic cultural golden age. Making it uniquely American and indispensable to its future". They believe this new age not only invented the Broadway musical. But gave the world jazz, blues and many new forms of performing and visual arts to appeal to the masses. If you are interested you can become a member here : http:// www.coneyisland.com

## Only in America.....

Lucy the Elephant is now Coney Island's most famous resident built in 1882. Weighing about 90 tons this animal shaped novelty was built to attract real estate investment and tourists.

After falling into disrepair in the 1960s a "Save Lucy" campaign was set-up to refurbish her and in 1976 she became a National Historic Landmark. In 2006 she was struck by lightening and her tucks went black. Poor Lucy!

The Coney Island Polar Bear Club consists of a group of people who swim in the freezing waters through the winter months, most notably on New Year's Day. Bonkers!

# USA VOTED - TOP 6 'OTHER' LETTER "C" DESTINATIONS ...

**Clearwater, Florida**
Distance to Saint Petersburg Clearwater Airport is 10 miles or approx. 20mins.

**Colorado Springs, Colorado**
Distance from Colorado Springs Airport is 7 miles or approx. 23mins.

**Chattanooga, Tennessee**
Distance from Huntsville airport 120 miles or 2hrs 15mins.

**Christmas, Missouri & Florida**
Distance to Sawyer airport is 46 miles or 1 hour.

**Cape Cod, Massachusetts**
Cape Cod Airport to Central Cape Cod is 13miles or approx. 20 mins.

**Cape Canaveral, Florida**
Orlando International Airport to Cape Canaveral is 46miles or approx. 50mins

# D *is for......* Daytona

**Daytona 500, Florida -** The State of Florida, a Playground for Adults. Welcome Race Fans greets you everywhere at Daytona Beach. "Nothing Like the Taste of Adrenaline to Know that You're Alive !"

"D" is for Daytona Beach, Florida. For those of you who have never been to America and have no idea where to start, then I you can't go far wrong if you go anywhere in Florida. Its like a Playground for Adults!

Of course it is well known for its theme parks, cheap flights and plenty to do. But I think of the State of Florida as "one huge theme park" catering for all ages. With fantastic year-round weather (avoiding hurricane season of course) and the added bonus of only being a car journey away from your next fun destination in any direction.

I had hundreds of votes for destinations all across Florida. But the outright winner by a mile in the end was The Daytona 500 at Daytona Beach the National Headquarters of NASCAR. I was pre-warned about the stereo-typical beer swilling, red-neck American's who attend but being English and knowing little about car racing, I knew it was going to be an experience regardless of the race itself.

The nature of my A to Zee journey meant I never had much time for pre-planning and research. But on this occasion, for those of you who are seriously thinking of going to the Daytona Races definitely try to book tickets and accommodation early. There are events throughout the year and a wide variety of ways to enjoy them from VIP, RV-ing to tail-gating. Check out this website: www.daytona500.com.

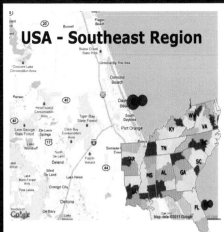

**USA - Southeast Region**

If like me, you just find yourself arriving on the day of the 500 (usually in late February) then my advice would be to get to the racetrack super early. Walk, cycle, taxi, car and certainly not (like me) in a memorabilia-clad RV.

Don't rely on the stewards or police officer's knowledge outside the track because many are brought in from out-of-town for the day so can be as clueless as you.

Critically, make sure you know exactly which queue to join beforehand. Or you can find yourself in a queue for 2 hours, then get turned around and join another because you went to the wrong entrance. Doh!

# Daytona Beach, Florida

One thing to note is that the airport (Daytona Beach International Airport) is right next door to the racetrack so worth a cab ride to get you within walking distance.

The final cardinal sin is to forget where you parked after the race, the amount of people just aimlessly walking around for hours in the dark trying to find their vehicle was amusing.

Just for the record - I made all of these mistakes !

What made Daytona such a memorable experience for me, was the build-up to the race. What added to the excitement was the banners, flags, beer tents and bars saying "Welcome Race Fans". The testosterone and gasoline in the air was palpable.

The track itself holds over 169 thousand people so the population of Daytona Beach swells for the week long Daytona 500 races. Sensibly the knowledgeable Daytonian's generally attend the less busy and inexpensive (but equally impressive) trial laps or special event races which occur over the days before the main event. Or stick around until March and attend the equally crazy Bike Week where over 600,000 leather-clad, tattooed bikers roll into town.

So having finally arrived at the right entrance and made my way inside the race track. You will find a range of race day events and attractions and another good reason to arrive early.

Once seated you can enjoy the immensity of the entire event. To my great amusement I was sat high in the stands looking down on the crowd and race track. With the sun behind us there was a sea of red-necks beginning to form in the midday sun. Now "I get it", I thought to myself!

To my joy the event started with the immortal words "Start Your Engines Please" closely followed by the overhead roar of a military fly-pass as the massive crowd roared in appreciation. I noted someone's T-shirt in the crowd which summed up very nicely the spectacle "Nothing Like the Taste of Adrenaline to Know that You're Alive!"

Then somewhat sedately, the race started with the safety car and the brightly coloured NASCARs whizzing by.

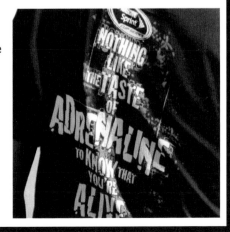

With the safety car dispersed and another roar from the crowd They're Off. Even being high in the stands and a good distance away from the track you could feel the force of the cars as they hurtled by. The noise was overwhelming with man and machine hitting speeds in excess of 180mph, it was spine tingling.

Making your way towards track side it becomes apparent that all that stands between you and certain death is a steel fence. Hence you are quickly dispersed by stewards or the police. The sheer noise, drag force and bullet fast speeds make you feel like you are going to be sucked onto the track.

# Daytona Beach , Florida

It also became clear why the lady I purchased my tickets from had sat me where I was. Sitting near the track without ear and eye defenders would be uncomfortable after only ten minutes.

So it's true the American red-necks have converted a no clue English girl into a NASCAR fan. I now "get" NASCAR and why it is so popular in many states across the US. I am now a self-confessed Petrol/Gas Head!

Even if you skip the speedway events, I was pleasantly surprised by Daytona Beach. It is clearly a motorsport mecca and a spring break party town for adults. But for me the most impressive part of Daytona Beach, was the beach itself.

Florida has it's famous South Beach home of the Miami Music festival. But having visited some of the world's famous beaches like Bondi, Sydney, Venice in California and Waikiki in Hawaii. Daytona Beach with its neighbouring Ormond and New Smyrna was one of the longest beaches I have ever seen in my life. You honestly you could not see from one end to the other.

Even more bizarre is the fact that they have a 23-mile two lane sand roadway at the top of it where cars, trucks, ice-cream vans and other random vehicles meander up and down it. Here tailgaters sit on their trucks and enjoy a BBQ, a few cool beers watching the plastic people go by.

Driving away from Daytona I would head west to downtown DeLand along the scenic St. Johns River.

Or to the south to New Smyrna Beach, affectionately known as Old Florida with it's pristine beaches and waterfronts. Or Edgewater nicknamed The Hospitality City with its friendly small-town quaintness.

For a taste of up-market Florida head north to Ormond Beach and Ormond-by-the-Sea. At the turn of the 20th century it was the hang-out of the rich and famous including The Casements, the former winter home of John D. Rockefeller.

So to conclude, I enjoyed the whole experience that was Daytona; from the racing, the location, the atmosphere and of course the weather. Eight million annual visitors a year can't be wrong!

Every time I visited the Sunshine State I always left with a big smile on my face and a longing to return soon.

## IF YOU HAVE MORE TIME ...

### Outdoors People

Why not create your own Daytona experience and have a race at Go Kart City, the largest track in the area. Or go looking for gators or endangered manatees, lots of companies offer airboat rides.

There are well over 40 golf clubs in the area, the Daytona Beach Golf Club has Scottish heritage. Designed by Donald Ross born in 1872 who has designed over 400 prestigious clubs across America. Daytona Beach is the National Headquarters of the Ladies Professional Golf Association as well as for Florida's Tennis Centre where you can enjoy excellent facilities a pro. shop as well as certified professional staff.

Ocean fishing can be done at Main Street Pier; rod, bait and reel rentals are available here. They can also advise on the numerous fishing competitions held in the area throughout the year.

### History, Culture & Gifts

Volusia Mall is one of Daytona's largest shopping destinations. Or check out Ocean Walk Shoppe's, a six-level oceanfront complex including a 10 screen movie theatre: www.oceanwalkshoppess.com. Daytona also has a Flea and Farmers market open Friday & Weekends 9am-5pm, check out: www.daytonafleamarket.com. Chocoholics should check out Angell & Phelps Chocolate Factory: www.angellandphelps.com.

I would recommend the following museums: the Museum of Arts and Sciences and The Williams Children's Museum-loads of fun and things to do for all the family. Unusually for a US museum it has a Cuban Art display as well as Americana memorabilia.

### Photographers (People & Places)

Take a scenic river tour to Ponce de Leon lighthouse and see the beautiful riverfront homes, dolphins and manatees. The lighthouse, just south of Daytona Beach, offers great views of the inter-coastal waterways and Atlantic. Built in 1887 the 176 foot tall lighthouse (Florida's tallest) is in a good state of repair with the original keepers dwellings.

For those feeling fit there are 203 steps to the top. By way of reference if you have ever had to climb them. There are 193 steps at Covent Garden, London, the Statue of Liberty has 357 and the Leaning Tower of Pisa has 294. Check out: www.ponceinlet.org

### Only in America.....

Close-by to Daytona check out Cassadaga, on the National Register of Historic Places, its a tiny community of practicing spiritualists. The Camp being the oldest active religious community in south-eastern US.

Or if you are searching for the Fountain of Youth? Head to DeLeon Springs named after Juan Ponce de Leon who discovered the Springs in 1513.

Darren Waltrip finally won the Daytona 500 after his 17th attempt in 1989. He drove car number 17 and had pit stall 17 that day.

Or weirder still, three hours south west of Daytona go Horse Surfing at Palma Sola Bay in Bradenton. It sounds cool, but to be honest it's a bit of a gimmick as you ride a horse into the water then try and stand-up on it. Don't think this will be in the Olympics any time soon!

# USA VOTED - TOP 6 'OTHER' LETTER "D" DESTINATIONS ...

### Disneyland, California
Distance to Los Angeles International Airport is 36 miles or approx. 45 mins.

### Death Valley, California
Distance to McCarran international airport is 130 miles or approx. 3hrs 30 mins.

### Dodge City, Kansas
Distance to Garden City airport is 40 miles or 47mins.

### Durango, Colorado
Distance to Four Corners airport is 40 miles or 1 hour.

### Deep Creek, Maryland
Distance to Baltimore airport is 100 miles or 2hrs 20mins.

### Dickel, Tennessee
Distance to Tullahoma Airport is 3 miles or 10mins.

*E is for......* **E**ureka Springs

**Eureka Springs, Arkansas** - America's Forgotten State, Welcome to Arkansas - where the greeting is as warm as the pristine waters and diverse people who live there. It's easily accessible, lots to do and fantastic weather year-round.

"E" is for Eureka Springs, Arkansas. I had lots and lots of "E" Votes but they tended to be one-off votes rather than a substantial number. Eureka came up a lot, but people generally didn't know the state. I was all ready to go the 1,000 miles north to New York and Ellis Island when Eureka just pipped it in the end. Admittedly I could have gone to Eureka, California, Missouri, Kansas or Illinois. But in the end I decided on Arkansas, for no other reason than I knew absolutely nothing about the State.

Arkansas is affectionately known as "The Natural State" and although one of the lesser known states in America, once you have visited you will be shouting "Eureka—I Have Found It". A state and place you will want to go back to again and again without necessarily being able to describe why? It kinda' grabs hold of you and won't let go.

A little-known fact is that Arkansas has the most diverse population of any state in the US. When I asked around on my journey it also seemed to be the state that most Americans know very little about. As one of the locals remarked (after a few beers) *"people normally end up here by accident because they are 'different' somehow (criminals, gays, teenage single mums) you name it. But we don't judge. If they too have an open mind and are willing to work hard, they're ALL welcomed"*.

I certainly felt welcome and at ease, come to think of it I have a few skeletons in my cupboard! Maybe that was why I liked Arkansas and Eureka Springs so much.

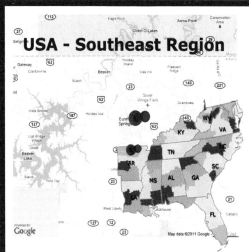

The Ozark Mountain region has a mild, year round climate. With spring coming in late February followed by long warm summer afternoons. Then autumn colours with a chance of snowfall make for an easy season shift.

If you like the Outdoors, especially water, then you'll like Arkansas. Hiking, inner-tubing, canoeing or kayaking in the warm waters is especially popular.

It also seems a good bikers spot, as I saw lots and lots of Harley Davidson's snaking there way around the mountains and quiet roads taking in the picturesque scenery.

# Eureka Springs, Arkansas

The Ozark Mountain and Buffalo National River region is normally where people land first. Fishing happens everywhere and anywhere there's water, luckily there's plenty of it in Arkansas. Water, water everywhere and thank goodness because the temperatures in the summer can top triple digits.

Places I would recommend to visit would be Newton County, which is the Elk capital of Arkansas. It hosts an annual Elk and Bluegrass Festival in June each year.

Or the Buffalo National Park & River, designated America's first National River it flows for more than 135 miles through the Ozarks and into the White River. I stopped off at Tyler Bend which had all the best facilities.

If you want to get out of the heat and into the water then I would recommend Norfolk Lake. It was so clean and has over 500 miles of unspoiled shoreline.

But my absolute favourite was nature's own water park called the Blue-Ribbon Creek. By nature, I mean it is a crystal clear meandering creek with sudden rapids that flow into deep pools surrounded by hills and lush pastures. Just like a man-made waterpark.

Not forgetting Arkansas Waterway State laws, which tell you to make sure your "floating vessel is not susceptible to swamping, tipping on rolling". Based upon the menagerie of inflatables I saw floating downstream I don't think these laws where always complied with!

Also check out the Diamond Region of Lakes With over 72,000 acres of wide open waters and 1,000 miles of shoreline it is perfect for a range of water activities. I loved the houseboats scattered around the lake. This whole area is great for accommodation, dining, shopping (especially Outfitters) and water rentals.

For you non swimmers, if it gets too hot, there is always the Blanchard Springs Caverns. More popularly known as the "Cosmic Cave" you can enjoy the stalagmite/tights to your hearts content. I'm not a big cave fan, so I thought it was a bit crap, but many of locals recommended it to me.

Heading to Eureka Springs itself, it is located in the far south west of Arkansas in the Ozark Mountain Region. Downtown you can enjoy a leisurely stroll down the streets enjoying the many shops and galleries.

Bang in the centre of downtown are two hotels Basin Park and the Crescent Hotel, which date back to the early 19th century and are famed for their ghost tours. As they put it "Some Guests Checked Out...But Never Left!" Wocka Wocka..!

To underline Arkansas "anything goes" mentality Eureka holds the following events annually: The Ozark Mountain Hoe-down & Jamboree. The Ozark UFO conference and The Great Passion Play which has the largest statue of Christ on the continent. All run from Spring onwards.

If you like Religion or Theology then you MUST see the Passion of Christ Play.

# Eureka Springs, Arkansas

Even if you don't, I would recommend you go and see it with some like-minded friends. Just to see how many times you can "Roll Your Eyes" at some of the things that happen, or to see how many people you can upset by starting an "evolution" conversation in the interval!

Just in case you are not convinced by now that Arkansas is a very liberal place then this should confirm it. Eureka Springs holds its annual Diversity Weekend in April. Described as *"a casual affair, in a casual and accepting environment, hoping to bring people together rather than place new barriers between them".* I think that's American for, there might be some gays?!

Personally I found myself drawn to The Show You've Got To See! American's don't do subtlety very well! ! It has had nightly shows running for 36 years at the Pine Mountain theatre. It you have experienced the Dixie Stampede it is a bit like that, without the Dolly Parton endorsement. All red, white and blue for the whole family as American as Apple Pie.

Side stepping the tourist traps and if you consider yourself eccentric at heart then you will probably like Mrs. Quigley's strange little castle. The house dates back to the early 1900's, when Elsie Quigley designed "a house that brought nature indoors". Inside it looks like the house plants have taken over, with tropical plants growing floor to the second story ceiling. Outside she also designed an amazing perennial garden with over 400 varieties of flowers. There is even somewhere to sleep in the treetops.

Eureka Springs as its name suggests, reminds you water is never far away. Blue Spring, spews 38 million gallons of cold, crystal-clear water a day for tourists to visit.

Also close-by is Beaver Lake and the White River. The White River (I think because of the smoky white mist it gives off in the mornings) offers record breaking trout fishing.

I found the water so pristine you could actually see the bottom from several feet above. I am sure it was no coincidence that this was one of the few places I actually caught any fish on my trip across the States. Five trout in fact, which I was very proud of. I smoked them that day and they tasted fantastic!

I loved Arkansas and felt it was America's Best Kept Secret. I visited it again and again because of its central location and outdoors lifestyle. But it is for its people that I will fondly remember Arkansas, their openness and lack of pretence make it a pretty special place to hang out in. Not forgetting of course, its delicious trout!

# IF YOU HAVE MORE TIME ...

## Outdoors People

Eureka Springs is surrounded by three rivers (Kings, Buffalo & White) and two lakes (Beaver & Table Rock) perfect for boating, canoeing, rafting or kayaking. I would head to the Riverview Resort, here they provide you everything you will need for a day out canoeing on the water. Dropping you at one end of the White River with a map, some food and then pick you up later in the day.

A pre-booked fishing trip is also a must, there are many suppliers in the area so I would suggest doing your own research.

If you want to take in the scenery on a hike then I would recommend Hobbs or Devil's Den State Park. Or if you're a mountain biker then check out Lake Leatherwood Park and research the Fat Tire festival held in July annually.

## History, Culture & Gifts

The City of Eureka Springs was founded and named on July 4, 1879. Today, it is listed on the National Register of Historic Places. Downtown Eureka Springs is definitely worth a visit as it has some unique and lovely shops to meander around. If you get chance, have a drink or lunch at the Crescent Hotel first opened in 1886 it is a very good example of Victorian architecture and nice food too.

Set in 120 acres of forest, gardens and sculptures you may want to take in the Crystal Bridges Museum of American Art. Outside it is one of the most beautiful art galleries I have ever visited across the world. It has a collection made up of Colonial, 19th Century, Modern and Contemporary works.

## Photographers (People & Places)

Roaring River State Park has over 3,000 acres of the most rugged and scenic terrain of anywhere in the southwest Ozarks. Or to the North West is Withrow Springs State Park providing scenic mountains outlooks and valleys along the War Eagle River. My final recommendation would be to take a trip along the Buffalo River by bike, hike or canoe. The River starts as a trickle in the Boston Mountains and eventually ends up as a rushing river in the Buffalo State Park, Arkansas.

Also worth a visit, just because of the sheer size of it, is the Statue of Christ. Which impressively stands 7 stories high and can be seen for miles around.

## Only in America ...

Built in 1980, for a contemporary and environmental approach to Religion you should check out Thorncrown Chapel. The best way to describe it is "an inside out church" set in a grove of trees in a woodland. Architecturally stunning.

If you're a self-professed Geek, check out Geographic's, a shop in downtown Eureka Springs. They produce T-shirts in these design categories (wait for it...) Geology, Dinosaurs, Chemistry, Biology, Computer Geek-ology and Other Ology's. My personal favourite being "Computer Programmers do it Byte by Byte " Cheesy! Or "Other Than That Mrs. Lincoln, How Did You Like The Play?". Cummon' they will have spent weeks racking their nerdy brains to come up with those!

# USA VOTED - TOP 6 'OTHER' LETTER "E" DESTINATIONS ...

**Ellis Island, New York**
Distance to Newark Airport is 10 miles or approx. 20mins.

**Eugene, Oregon**
Mahlon Sweet Field Airport to Eugene is 10 miles or approx. 21mins.

**Eden, Utah**
Distance to Salt Lake City airport is 64 miles or 1 hour 20mins.

**Ely, Minnesota**
Distance to Duluth airport is 106 miles or 2hrs.

**Egg Harbour, Wisconsin**
Distance to Austin Straubel Airport is 72 miles or 1hr 30mins.

**Elkhart, Indiana**
Elkhart Municipal Airport is 4 miles or 12mins.

*F is for......*

Franklin

**Franklin, Tennessee -** Site of one of the bloodiest battles of the American Civil War.

With Nashville, Graceland and the Jack Daniel's Distillery just down the road.

Tennessee certainly is the All American State.

"F" is for Franklin, Tennessee. When it came to Voting many Tennessee natives were disappointed that I couldn't have Nashville, Memphis or Graceland in the book. They felt this was a travesty, undeterred they voted for Franklin instead. The fact that it is home to one of the bloodiest Civil War battles and has the Jack Daniels and George Dickel Distilleries down the road also made it a popular choice.

So in honour of my Tennessee friends who in essence "fixed" my voting system, I felt I should honour their requests and briefly mention their first choices, before covering Franklin. So lets start with "The King" and Graceland.

If the Grand Canyon had not got the highest Votes for "G" then Graceland would have won. It is a great place to visit, I thoroughly enjoyed it. I have to admit to not being a huge Elvis fan, I like the guy, but I wouldn't say I own many of his albums. I was however married by Elvis at the White Wedding Chapel in Vegas, so he holds a warm place in my heart.

Walking around Graceland can be quite amusing because it is like stepping back in time noseying into a garish 1970s home. With plush wall to ceiling carpets, plastic furniture and brightly coloured bathrooms. You only need to picture your own childhood or a recent retro movie to imagine the scene.

I went on the VIP tour of Graceland which I would highly recommend. I was lucky enough to go on the tour alone, so I got to see some extra special things.

In true Elvis style, all the tour guides are all friends, acquaintances or people who knew Elvis personally when he was alive. To them his legacy continues and they enjoy telling you their own little personal stories about him. For example, I was shown a bright pink bathroom upstairs and was told this was where Elvis was found dead.

Out of respect to his friend, I avoided the inappropriate question I was thinking "Is it true he was found on the toilet?"

# Franklin, Tennessee

I was then taken to the back of the house to one of his garages and a purple convertible Cadillac. The story goes that the Cadillac was originally white. One day whilst Elvis was hanging out with some of his buddies, some blueberries rolled down the hood of the car. Elvis squashed them and said "Man, I think I like this colour. Hey guys, what do you think of this colour?" The Cadillac was painted "blueberry purple" the very next day. How cool was Elvis?

The other surprising thing about Elvis's house are the rooms upon rooms upon rooms full of gold discs, costumes and photographs of him with world figures. It is almost overwhelming, it's like he was some kind of a God!

The shrine towards the end is respectful, peaceful and nicely done. As you stand there with people sobbing you realize to some people, he really was like a God.

But the absolute best thing for me, was as you stepped out into his back yard. It is like stepping out into anybody's back yard. The only difference was, in Elvis's there are two 737 airplanes! I was so gob-smacked I went back into the kitchen, wiped my eyes and went back out again to double check what I had just seen.

And as if that wasn't enough, you can visit inside one of them, the Lisa Marie. Which is like a nightclub with numerous lounges, bars, dance floors and lots and lots of beds! "Urr Huh !"

Inside Elvis had 24 carat gold seat belts specially fitted. The tail-fin of his plane has the acronym "TCB" with a lightening bolt on it. Which stands for "Takin' Care of Business". That for me summed up Graceland and Elvis - legend!

As for Nashville and Memphis they are both fantastic places to visit. If you are a frequent US traveller and have done all the usual San Francisco, New York, Chicago, Orlando and Vegas destinations. Then these two cities should be your next "must-see's".

Memphis is a bit rougher than Nashville, but as a result a night out on Beale Street is a lot wilder. Unsurprisingly Memphis plays Soul & Blues and Nashville, Country. Or "Cuntrie", as they call it!

Nashville is the home of the Grand Ol' Opry a famous US gospel and country venue. By contrast Memphis has all the old rock 'n' roll, blues and swing studios. Interestingly if you end up visiting both, you will find that both lay claim to being the Birthplace of the Blues.

Although Nashville is a pretty big city, the main parts of it are all downtown so I would recommend taking a walking tour. I was lucky enough to get shown around by a Nashville native. Whose generations have lived and grown-up in the area, Brenda Kay of Gray Line tours.

# Franklin, Tennessee

What she didn't know about Nashville wasn't worth knowing! She took us inside the Grand Ol' Opry, famous Tootsie's bar as well as an old press printers, Hatch Show Print. It is claimed that it is bad luck if a Presidential candidate doesn't have some of their campaign posters printed there.

If I had to pick between Memphis and Nashville, I would pick Nashville. There are more places to visit in the surrounding areas and the history about the Civil War is prevalent. Although there are festivals and events everywhere in Tennessee, I think Nashville would be a good base and Memphis you could stop off at on a weekend.

But, I did like Memphis as well, here I did all the sites on a Rock 'n' Roll Tour Bus where the guide sings his way around the city. We took in Sun Records and the other notable rock 'n' roll stop-offs like recording studios and birthplaces.

That night I spent on Beale Street, if you have been to New Orleans it is on a par with Bourbon Street. It is a two-sided main street full of bars, clubs and restaurants playing every kind of music.

I had the pleasure of meeting Melody, the wife of Blind Mississippi Morris when I arrived at BB King's on Beale Street. Morris was singing and playing on stage which is how we got talking.

Originally from Tuscumbia in Alabama, Morris has been playing the rhythm and blues clubs for around 50 years and is pretty famous in these parts. Everywhere we went, everybody knew him.

He told me stories of many famous jazz, soul and blues friends including BB King himself. I spent the afternoon and evening with them enjoying their stories from back in the day when rock 'n' rock was being born in Memphis.

Needless to say how I got home that night is a little vague. Apart from I had a signed Blind Mississippi Morris CD in my pocket and a T-shirt on that said "What Happens on Beale Street, Stays On Beale Street!"

Moving swiftly on, I have to give a special mention to a newly opened restaurant I visited for a fine dining experience called -The Flight Restaurant.

I had the tasting menu which came with wine recommendations. It has a really unusual menu showcasing many American classics, but with a fine dining twist. We had a raucous night, the food and company were excellent until the wee hours.

So back to Franklin after my little detour around Tennessee.

The City of Franklin was founded in 1799 named after Benjamin Franklin. Much of the architecture of the era still remains on the main downtown streets.

Franklin is most famous for its Civil War Heritage. I had visited many Civil War sites on my tour across America like Gettysburg, Chickamauga, Georgia as well as a handful in Virginia but they didn't seem to capture my imagination as much as the battles that had occurred in Tennessee.

# Franklin, Tennessee

I think this was because in Tennessee the entire State was caught up in the unfolding events. Brother, father, mother and daughter became embroiled in the horror and needlessness of war.

For those of you not familiar with the American Civil War (different to American War of Independence) here is a brief overview.

The war was fought between the Northern States (Union or Yankees) led by Ulysses S. Grant and the Southern States (Confederates or Rebels) by Robert E. Lee in 1861-1865.

The North wanted the South to give up their large plantations, cotton & tobacco farms and instead build factories, abolish slavery and move towards a centralized federal government. It was triggered by the election to President of Abraham Lincoln in 1860, who favoured the North's view.

The first shots were fired by Confederate troops at the Union stronghold Fort Sumter, Charleston on April 12th, 1861.

There would be more than 620,000 killed (2% of the population at the time) and over 375,000 injured during the war. The most infamous of the battles being Gettysburg because it was the bloodiest and seen as the turning point for the war.

General Lee of the Confederates surrendered to Grant on the 9th April 1854. Five days later Lincoln was assassinated.

The Battle of Franklin was fought on November 30, 1864. It was one of the worst disasters of the war for the Confederate States Army (the South).

Confederate Lt. Gen. John Bell Hood's Army of Tennessee conducted numerous frontal assaults against fortified positions occupied by the Union forces under Maj. Gen. John M. Schofield of the Army of Tennessee. The Confederate assault with eighteen brigades of almost 20,000 men. Sometimes called the Pickett's Charge of the West, resulted in almost 10,000 casualties (killed, wounded, captured and missing).

Turning forty-four buildings in the town into make-shift field hospitals. With the first fifteen minutes being reported as the most bloody fifteen minutes in all of American history.

Critically for future battles, the Tennessee Army had lost numerous of its leaders including 14 Generals (killed, wounded or captured) and 55 regimental commanders. With Union deaths only being 189.

Despite this momentous effort Hood's Confederates, The Army of Tennessee, was unable to break through the Union lines. So Hood decided to retreat and hold control in Franklin until the morning when they could attack again.

# Franklin, Tennessee

Schofield (Union) in the meantime had been ordered by his commanding officer Thomas, not to counter attack and to retreat his troops to meet his in the north for future battles.

This presented Hood and the Army of Tennessee with a tough decision. Whether to retreat and risk the army dissolving through desertions, or to advance and face the might of the strengthened Union army in the north.

With no reinforcements available, Hood advanced his 26,500 man force against the Union army now combined with Schofield under Thomas towards Nashville.

On December the 15-16th strongly outnumbered and exposed to the elements, Hood was attacked by Thomas and defeated decisively. Hood's army were pursued aggressively forcing them to retreat to Mississippi with just under 20,000 men. The Army of Tennessee never fought again and Hood's career was ruined.

This became known as a pivotal moment in the civil war, which is why it is still remembered today at Franklin.

In memory of this momentous event you can still visit The Carter House, which was located at the center of the Union position.

Covering about 15 acres the house and outbuildings still show the scars of the battles. The Carter Family Garden, was also part of the Franklin battle site seeing tremendous fighting.

The nearby Carnton Plantation, home to the McGavock family during the battle, was one of the largest make-shift field hospitals and is open to the public today. Not only is it stooped in history, but it is also a fantastic example of a Planation for the era (ala) Gone with the Wind. As well as Will Lotz House which is now a Civil War House Museum.

Once you know the history of the place, those of you feeling alittle braver may want to visit the McGavock Confederate Cemetery. It is America's largest private federal cemetery and has the remains of 1,481 soldiers killed in the battle of Franklin.

Adjacent to that is a city park which was the site of the actual battle. It felt quite weird being there because to look at it you would have no idea that thousands of people had lost their lives there. It's true what they say "War, Brings Only to the Undertaker!"

# F is for......

# Franklin

Continuing the Civil War theme you can follow the path along Old Tennessee-the Settlers to Soldiers Trail. This takes in some of Tennessee most beautiful scenery on the outskirts of famous civil war sites.

The Trail takes you on a large circular tour from Mount Pleasant in the South through Columbia, Spring Hill

and Franklin to the north. Then back down south past Leiper's Fork, Bethel, Williamsport and Canaan.

These areas are famous for being where all the Country Stars have their million dollar homes when they are in Tennessee.

I thought it was amazing as it takes you through some of Tennessee's most beautiful countryside and grandiose houses. Surrounded by deep valleys, small middle-class country towns with horse ranches everywhere.

Of course, whilst in the area you must take in the two famous American Distilleries, George Dickel and Jack Daniel's. I am not a big whiskey fan, but thought I should go and check out these classic American bourbons.

The town of Tullahoma is home to the George Dickel distillery tour. Here you can tour the distillery and discover their award -winning whiskey in the time honoured tradition.

VOTED FOR BY THE AUTHOR

BEST IN AMERICA

Flight Seafood Martini Restaurant, S. Main Street Memphis

Or around a 20 minute drive from Dickel is the world famous Jack Daniels Distillery in Lynchburg, where they make every drop of Jack.

Hold the bourbon for a minute, I had a nasty surprise awaiting me. You take the tour, see how it's all made, meet the people who make it, then just as you think you will walk into the tasting room you find out that Lynchburg is a "dry" county! You can't taste a drop! Would you believe it!

If that happened at the Guinness Factory in Dublin it could very well start a riot!

So that was Franklin, Tennessee combined with Nashville, Memphis and the nearby Dickel and Jack Daniels distilleries. It is the perfect mix of culture, history, music and laughter.

The State is absolutely packed with things to do in every direction. Such friendly people and hospitality everywhere you go.

Places like Leipers Fork with its lush countryside, ranches and plantation feels like you're in a Gone With the Wind era.

Hey don't forget, Elvis was a smart guy and had travelled the world. He could have built Graceland anywhere, but he chose Tennessee.

You can't get a better endorsement than that!

# IF YOU HAVE MORE TIME ...

## Outdoors People

Close-by to downtown Franklin is the very impressive Vanderbilt Legends Golf Club. Which is a huge golf facility featuring a 36 hole course, a 19 acre practice facility, clubhouse and golf shop.

I would do further research on the Natchez Parkway which is a 444 mile National scenic by-way which closely follows the ancient trail travelled for centuries by tradesmen and Native Americans from Natchez in Mississippi to Nashville. The Natchez Trace Parkway is one of only six All American Roads covering 3 of America's most beautiful States. Coming off the driving route you can experience trail driving, hiking, biking, horseback riding and camping in some beautiful scenery.

## History, Culture & Gifts

The Tennessee Civil War Trail program is part of a 5 State trails system that invites you to visit Civil War sights. With more than a thousand places to visit they tell the epic and heartfelt stories of civilians and soldiers who experienced triumph and tragedy during the war. You can get more information at: www.civilwartrails.org.

Sometimes forgotten it was nice to come across a museum that chronicled the struggles, triumphs and significant contributions of the African-Americans during the Civil War. The tiny McLemore Museum in Franklin built by a slave was certainly worth a visit for a different slant on the war.

## Photographers (People & Places)

When in Tennessee you are surrounded by lush pastures, horses and everything Cuntrie! So for the perfect Gone with the Wind setting head to Leipers Fork which offers some of the best renovated plantation and antebellum houses this side of the Mississippi. Oh Ashley !

But Tennessee is most famous for the Great Smokey Mountains which hug the state's eastern border and the Appalachian Trail towards the Cumberland Gap. All these areas are famed for their Autumnal glows and rising mists first thing in the morning. Specifically I would check out the Cherokee National Forest and Clay State Park using Iron Mountain or Chattanooga as your base for all these sights.

## Only in America.....
Franklin holds a number of annual events including St Patrick's Day Brew Fest on Main Street when you can taste more than 40 beers and Irish whiskeys. The Franklin Rodeo rolls into town each Spring featuring steer wrestling, bronco and bull riding. Then in the Fall you can enjoy Pumpkin Fest and Civil War Re-enactments.

"Everybody Needs a Bit of Dolly in Their Lives" so why not head to Sevierville, hometown of the legend that is Dolly Parton. Brenda Kay, my native Tennessean tour guide, knew the family well and told me that she is absolutely tiny at about 5ft tall. Also that Dolly's husband Carl Dean is "Show Businesses Best Kept Secret" they have been married for decades but nobody really knows who he is. He is rarely seen in public and has only ever attended 1 of her performances.

# USA VOTED - TOP 6 'OTHER' LETTER "F" DESTINATIONS ...

**Fort Lauderdale, Florida**
Distance from Downtown to Fort Lauderdale
International Airport is 5 miles or 10mins.

**Flagstaff, Arizona**
Distance to Phoenix Sky Harbour Airport is 150 miles
or approx. 2hrs 30mins.

**Fargo, North Dakota**
Hector International Airport is 5 miles or 12mins.

**Fort Knox, Kentucky**
Louisville International Airport is 42 miles or 45mins.

**Fort Worth, Texas**
Dallas/Fort Worth International Airport to Downtown
Fort Worth is 33 miles or approx. 36mins.

**Fredericksburg, Virginia**
Ronald Reagan Airport to Fredericksburg is 52 miles
or 1hr.

# $G$ is for......

# $G$rand Canyon

**Grand Canyon, Arizona -** The Grand Canyon State Park encompasses over two thousand square miles. Top to bottom the canyon drops over six thousand feet. I think the Grand Canyon is why the American word "Awesome" was invented !

"G" is for the Grand Canyon, Arizona. There has been plenty written about the Grand Canyon so rather than give you the in-depth detail on it I will give you the basics. The nature of my backwards and forwards journey meant I actually went past it many times and visited it more than 5 times in all kinds of weather.

The Grand Canyon is actually a recognized State Park that covers over a 1,904 square miles. To put that into context it would roughly be the equivalent in size to the City of New York and London combined. If you hiked 5 miles every single day, it would take you over a year to hike the entire Grand Canyon.

Most people however measure the canyon in river miles (277m) along the course of the Colorado River beginning at Lees Ferry and ending at the Grand Wash Cliffs. Which if you rafted it, would take over 2 weeks.

But it is the drop for which the canyon is most famous for, from the bottom of the canyon floor to the top of the rim it is around 6,000 feet. Or 6 Eiffel Towers or 7 Seattle Space Needles piled one on top of the other.

So even though I visited it 5 times in many different ways, in reality even I only saw a small fraction of this huge canyon.

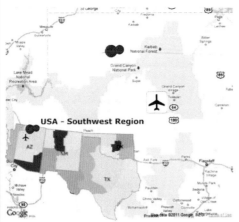

USA - Southwest Region

The Grand Canyon is thought to have been formed 2 billion years ago when the movement of a plate carrying the island arcs collided with a plate that eventually became North America.

It is the subsequent geological events and then 5 million years of erosion caused by the Colorado River which created the Colorado plateau. As the Colorado River cuts down from the Rocky Mountains to the Gulf of California, so the canyon deepens. Erosion carves faster and layers collapse, eventually forming the unique colourful slope profiles that make up the Grand Canyon.

# Grand Canyon, Arizona

For more information about the geology of the place. Check out: Grand Canyon National Park Service.

Ok, so when visiting the Grand Canyon there are a few things to do before setting off. Firstly, check the weather before you go, especially if you are planning on just going for the day. The varying elevations and climate means if you are not careful it can be the "Grand Mist Canyon" and you won't see anything, making it a wasted journey.

Second, if time is not an issue, I would highly recommend The Grand Circle tour instead, which includes the Grand Canyon. It has the best USA scenery across 5 different states. Check out: www.grandcircle.org.

There have obviously been many books, websites, brochures (etc.) that cover the Grand Canyon so I won't bore you with Wikipedia-type facts. What I will do instead is give you my own personal recommendations based upon my many visits.

From my experience, generally speaking there seems to be 4 "types" of visitor to the Grand Canyon as follows the:

- Just to say "You've Seen It" visitor.
- "The Griswold's" - got all the gear family.
- The young, fit, "Adrenaline Junkie".
- "Once in a Lifetime" special occasional people.

I will cover these in turn.

## Just to say "You've Seen It" Visitor

Here are my 3 best ways to experience the Canyon in a Fast-Food Style:

**1) Helicopter from Vegas** - if you're already in Vegas, take a helicopter trip over the Canyon. You get to see the sheer vastness of the space including the Hoover Dam. Reasonable pictures and it is all done in about half a day, so you can get back to the tables! If you think you are afraid of helicopters, trust me, don't be. I have been in about 5 now in 4 different States and they are not as scary as you might think.

**2)** Get yourself to **The Skywalk, Nevada**. Everyone thinks this is at the Grand Canyon Park, but it is not. You can walk out over the Canyon on a clear glass platform and look down. Yikes!

**3) Drive through the Park** - Most people stay the night before in Flagstaff. "Don't" its rubbish. Instead I would recommend staying at Page, Glen Canyon or my personal favourite Lake Powell. If you plan to spend the whole day at the Canyon check the weather the night before.

Your navigation system or GPS may be a little temperamental. If this happens to you, pop in Grand Canyon Airport or Village instead. Can you believe TOM TOM and Garmin couldn't find the Grand Canyon for goodness sake!

# The Grand Canyon, Arizona

On the way there do not be tempted by signs that say "North or South Rim or Viewing Area" just keep going to the Park itself. Pay your entry fee and then drive from viewing point to viewing point. The first one is pretty much immediately after you have arrived in the park.

Although it is a pain stopping and starting, I would recommend stopping at every single one. Honestly it is worth it, each one offers a very different view. Just as you think you cannot be "wowed" anymore you turn a corner, pull in and find yourself awestruck again.

The visitors centre is definitely worth a visit and there is a small bus terminal. Take advantage of this if you can, so you don't have to worry about parking in the little lay-bys. Or alternatively, if you are brave, you could cycle it. But remember it is 150 miles long and will take a good couple of hours.

Ok that's it, Grand Canyon Fast Food-Style. Boom!

### The Griswold's

Ok, so you are probably a family who likes to research everything before you arrive. You have booked well in advance on the camp grounds and have got "all the gear". You probably intend on spending a week at the Canyon, you will cycle, hike it and the whole family will just enjoy the experience once the crowds have subsided in the evenings.

This is possible but does take a lot of pre-planning and booking in advance. You will need think through the types of activities you will want to do to and have the relevant maps, licenses and equipment.

But hey, you're The Griswold's you don't need me to tell you that!

I would not say this is your average camping break because the terrain can be tough and the temperatures very variable because of the elevations.

The Park Service can provide you with a detailed Grand Canyon Guide prior to your arrival which contains things to do and Ranger-led programs (young and old). So I would encourage you to get hold of one of these before arriving in order to plan your visit. You normally pick this up on the day as you arrive, or at the Visitor's Centre. But I am sure they will send them out beforehand if you ask. Just make sure your brochure matches the Season of your trip, as they change it.

So once you are there and all set-up, take it in at your own pace and enjoy all that pre-work you had to do. It will be worth it in the end. You deserve it Clark!

# MON QUESTIONS

*How often do people fall over the edge*

◆
Surprisingly, people rarely fall over the edge. Those who do fall seldom survive the canyon's initial 300-foot sheer drop. Be careful and keep a safe distance from the edge.

## The Adrenaline Junkie

Most adrenaline junkies will immediately think **White Water Rafting**. All of these types of activities are limited so you need to have a lot of spare cash and be booking around a year in advance.

But be warned, it is more like drifting than thrashing around in white waters. Plus it can take 6 -14 days to raft the Grand Canyon and once you are in it, it can be pretty difficult to get out of it. So if it is your first time and you "don't like it" you are screwed! Be prepared to be petrified or bored for the next 5 days or arrange (at your expense) a helicopter out!

# The Grand Canyon, Arizona

Personally I would recommend white water rafting at Big Water, Page or Green River instead to see if you like it, without getting stuck. I did try Green River and found this to be much more challenging and fun than doing the Canyon itself.

**Horse Riding** - can be done but there are limited companies that do it and you normally have to book it in a package with a hotel. Normally they don't offer overnight outside camping, but they do take you through some great scenery on a 1 or 2 hour ride. Not mention it is much comfier than the "mule" alternative.

**Donkey/ Mule Rides** - for me this was the scariest of the lot! You meet at silly o'clock in the morning at the South Rim.

I am not knocking it and I'm sure some people love it, but 6-hours on the back of a donkey is not my idea of fun. I am not exactly light (you are weighed) so I am sure unpleasant for the donkey as well!

The slippery trek and plummeting sheer drops had me holding on for dear-life. This had gone beyond adrenaline to "pure fear!" Never again! Poor (Dominic The..) Donkey!

**Mountain Biking** - you can't really mountain bike in the Grand Canyon Park itself, except on the roadways. So instead you'll need to cross out of the Grand Canyon National Park into the Kaibab National Forest which borders the park on both the North and South Rim.

On the North Rim avid cyclists flock to the Rainbow Rim Trail, an 18-mile stretch of single track (no motor vehicles allowed). Its remoteness allows unique access to five canyon overlooks. I didn't do it personally, but heard very good things about it from people who had.

Alternatively old logging roads, jeep trails and footpaths crisscross the North Rim providing more cycling routes. You can get more information about biking at the Kaibab Plateau Visitor Centre in Jacob Lake.

**Bungee Jumping** - before you get excited you cannot officially bungee jump in the Grand Canyon Park. However it has been done unofficially at Navajo Bridge at Marble Canyon which spans across the Colorado River right over the Grand Canyon. You'll need your own rope and a good look-out. Good luck!

As I said I don't think this is "officially legal", so be warned. If you want to see it being done, then type in Navajo Bridge Bungee on You-Tube and you can see the adrenaline nutters there!

From experience I would suggest if you are an adrenaline junkie that maybe the Grand Canyon is not for you. The Canyon is about stopping and taking it all in. When you are concentrating on "holding on" you don't get to see the Canyon it all its glory.

# The Grand Canyon, Arizona

Instead I would recommend going to other States like Colorado, Utah or Arkansas for your adrenaline fix.

### "Once in a Lifetime"-Special Occasions

Marriage at the Grand Canyon - these tend to occur at the Grand Canyon Ranch. I didn't see one, so I cannot really comment. But I think the destination alone would make it a great and probably a very expensive experience. www.grandcanyonranch.com/ romantic_getaways.htm

For a slightly cheaper alternative, get hitched in Vegas and then get an experienced photographer or helicopter company to take you to all the best spots at the canyon. Check out: www.grandcanyonphotography.com

**Float Down the Colorado** - Although away from the Canyon itself I would highly recommend a leisurely float down the Colorado River from Lake Powell through Glen Canyon then stop off at Kanab, Utah. You can hire a range of craft to do this, ask around at Lake Powell someone should be able to accommodate your requests.

**Hot Air Ballooning** - before booking this activity be sure to check exactly where your hot air balloon will venture as many cannot go near the Grand Canyon itself as there are strict restrictions. I had to pay for a private tour, but it was well worth it. The tranquillity of the balloon was the best way to enjoy the Arizona landscape without the whirring helicopter blades, strenuous activity or the congested commute of the park itself.

Normally timed around dawn and dusk when the wind speeds are friendliest the balloon glides up with the grace of a ballerina and before you can say "I'm afraid of heights" you are already high up in the air.

You can enjoy the peace and calmness of the ride and take in all the sites and colours at a leisurely pace.

This was truly amazing and by-far my favourite way to see the Canyon. If you're going to do this though, make sure you do it last. Try all the other ways to see the Canyon first so you can fully appreciate it.

So that is my whistle stop tour of the Grand Canyon, having experienced in many different ways and during many seasons.

If it is not on your Bucket List then it should be. American's use the "AWESOME" a lot and it beautifully sums up the experience that is The Grand Canyon.

## Outdoors People

I would check out the Arizona Trail, it is a 800-mile remote back country pathway that weaves its way border to border through some of Arizona's most spectacular scenery starting at Lake Jacob or Patagonia. The trail links National Parks, forests, deserts, mountains, canyons and historic places for you to hike, bike or ride. Visit: www.aztrail.org.

Also popular is the Kaibab National Forest those 1.6 million acres straddles the Grand Canyon with ecosystems ranging from Desert to Alpine. Its wonderful for mountain biking, trail-riding and hiking in the summer. Or if you fancy a bit of cross-country skiing and snowboarding then you should head to the North Rim in the winter.

For just pure fun with friends spend the day tubing down the Salt River in silly inflatables. Contact: Salt River Recreation, Mesa, Arizona.

## History, Culture & Gifts

Want to get insight on how wealthy frontier families lived in the 1900s, then you should visit Riordan Mansion State historic Park which provides tours of this massive house. Or you may come across Pipe Spring National Monument. If you take the tour, it gives you an insight into early pioneer and religious life in the early 1800s.

Dating back even further is Sunset Crater and the Wupatki National Monument. Sunset Crater was born in a series of eruptions sometime between around AD 1040. Lava flows and cinders still look as fresh and rugged as the day they formed, providing a 1-mile loop trail through this amazing volcanic landscape. At the Wupatki National Monument - you can visit more than 800 ruins of the ancient homes and villages of the Singagua and Ancestoral Puebloans.

## Photographers (People & Places)

It appears on many PC screensavers, check out The Wave which you can find at Paria Wilderness, or see Havusu Falls for your own personal screensaver.

On a similar theme hire a boat at Dangling Rope Marina and go to Rainbow Bridge National Monument. It is 275 feet across and 290 feet high and is the world's largest natural bridge -nearly as tall as the Statue of Liberty.

Rainbow Bridge may also be reached by trails across the Navajo nation, but permits are required as this area is sacred. You can get more information at the Navajo National Parks and Recreation Department.

## Only in America.....

I would recommend skipping the 'traditional' Grand Canyon stop-off of Flagstaff which I found quite dreary and do Bisbee to Sedona, then onto to the Grand Canyon. The town of Bisbee was founded in the late 1800s nested in the mile-high Mule Mountains. It is like stepping into the set of an old cowboy movie. Make sure you pay a visit to Brewery Gulch which is bar on the main street which is like an old time saloon. Whip crack away, whip crack away, whip crack away...!

There are certain parts of the Grand Canyon that remain sacred to Native American traditions, the Hualapai Tribe opened up their life to the public in 1988. Well worth a visit, you can get more information at: www.hualapaitourism.com.

# USA VOTED - TOP 6 'OTHER' LETTER "G" DESTINATIONS ...

### Glacier National Park, Montana
Distance from Glacier National Park International Airport is 24 miles or 39mins.

### Gettysburg, Pennsylvania
Distance to Harrisburg International Airport is 45 miles or approx. 51mins.

### Graceland, Tennessee
Graceland to Memphis International Airport is 5 miles or approx. 12mins.

### Greenwich Village, New York
Distance to JFK Airport is 19 miles or approx. 30mins.

### Geneva (On The Lakes), New York
Greater Rochester International Airport is 59 miles or approx. 59mins.

### Grand Rapids, Michigan
Distance to Gerald Ford International Airport is 14 miles or approx. 30mins.

# H *is for......*  **H**earst Castle

**Hearst Castle, California -** Drive through Northern California, enjoying the scenic Pacific Coast Highway and 101 surrounded by vast redwood forests. Then marvel at the extravagant mansion of William Hearst. Ridiculously opulent, over-the-top even by Californian standards !

"H" is for Hearst Castle, California. Another surprising winner beating such destinations as Hollywood and Harlem. It was amazing how many people around the USA had heard of Hearst Castle, personally I had never heard of it. So in the my usual "no research, just turn-up" travel style I was pleasantly surprised as it was not what I expected at all.

Firstly, it was one of the few times I didn't have to drive thousands of miles from my previous destination. Grand Canyon, Arizona to Hearst was only a few days away, I felt so lucky; this never happened!

Second, I was soon to discover that the drive up the Californian coast would be the highlight of my trip, not necessarily the Castle itself. Circumstances meant I headed north from LA, so I could enjoy the coastal scenery of the Pacific Coast Highway, 101 and 1 Californian highways taking in Big Sur, Nappa, Monterey and San Francisco. The drive went from cities & beaches, to rugged coastline then out into fresh air, masses of redwood forests and small towns.

I guess it is called the Golden Coast for a reason, I think everyone should do this drive at least once in their lives. I would have loved to have done it back in the hay-day of Hollywood when Sinatra, Davis-Jnr and Judy were around.

I think Northern California is actually nicer than the Southern part of the State. There are not as many major cities and the coast hasn't been rammed full with multi-million dollar homes. I also liked the fact the weather was alittle more temperamental, mirrored in the landscape.

Heading inland away from the coast the landscape is filled with centuries old redwood trees nestling between small village-like towns. There are even redwood trees you can drive your car through.

Get onto the Pacific Highway 1 heading north away from LA and Santa Barbara and purposely try to get lost. Highway 1 goes all the way up to Monterey so don't worry you won't venture too far away from civilization.

# Hearst Castle, California

I am confident to say that you will encounter a different experience round every corner. Mysteriously I found that the places that you thought sounded quite nice, like Vandenberg Village or Isla Vista, were just a mellay of residential estates.

But that is kind of the point, you have to keep going from place to place to discover Northern California. It isn't just handed to you on a plate like southern parts of the State.

I have numerous recommendations but personally I really liked Lake Nacimiento, Morro Bay and Carmel. They offered stunning coastal scenery against the wooded backdrop of the San Luis Obispo, Tierra Redonda and Carmel Mountains.

Get your camera ready you can take a fantastic shot of the Morro Bay Rock as the sun sets. You can't miss it, it will suddenly appear 500ft high, a lone rock rising out of the sea when your drive down the highway.

Eventually at the end of Pacific Highway 1 you will arrive at Monterey. This has been a popular seaside spot for centuries with multi-million dollar homes and resorts dotted all around. It reminded me of Redondo and Manhattan Beach, CA if you are familiar with them, but nicer.

Ironically I was robbed here late one night, so understandably my view of it is alittle tainted.

Needless to say I gave my assailants my cash, but managed to save my cards and drivers licence. Goodbye Monterey, I won't be back anytime soon.

It is worth noting at this point that you are very close (4 hours away) from Yosemite National Park.

During my journey across the USA the letter "Y" had 2 front runners from the beginning; Yellowstone and Yosemite. I was lucky enough to visit both and would highly recommend a visit to Yosemite. I often had conversations with people about which they/I liked best. The general consensus seemed to be "both" for very different reasons.

Firstly Yosemite is significantly smaller so by definition there is not as much to see.

But of the other hand its compactness makes the viewing of it a lot easier. I would almost describe it as a mini-Yellowstone which makes it more palatable as a tourist. If you only have 1 National Park to see and are short on time, I would choose this one.

Yosemite has numerous waterfalls after the spring snow melt. The most famous being the Yosemite Falls made up of 3 separate falls, the Upper, the Middle Cascade, Lower and Bridalveil Falls. Not forgetting the spectacular Tunnel View, drawing your eye to the centre of the towering waterfall framed by granite rocks either side.

## Hearst Castle, California

The other beauty of Yosemite is that you have a lot more freedom to actually physically enjoy the park by hiking, biking, horse riding, rock climbing and fishing. Unlike Yellowstone whose pre-historic nature with its geysers, wildlife and hot mud pools makes some of these types of activities impossible.

So in summary if you are in the area I would definitely recommend a trip to Yosemite it was certainly one of

my favourite National Parks after Yellowstone and Zion, Utah.

Looking at the map Hearst Castle would have been my next stop, but I was enjoying Northern California so much I decided to keep going and would circle back when I ran out of things to see.

The next major city I encountered was San Jose. It was a very nice urbanized California city, possibly one of the nicest. Unlike many of them it has some beautiful architecture which stems back to its Spanish roots. Instead of the usual concrete which dawns other Californian cities over earthquake concerns.

Just down the road is silicon valley, estimated to have some of the most expensive real estate in the world. I looked into it and a 2 bedroom apartment in Silicone Valley will set you back a cool $1.5 million.

In case you where wondering, "No" silicon valley isn't worth a visit. Because there is no real centre or hub, the buildings are really spread out in what feels like random neighbourhoods. Alternatively I did have fun sitting in some of the local coffee shops playing "Crazy Nerds" my own version of Angry Birds.

Self-confessed super geek David McClure who was involved in the setting-up many start-ups explains "Silicon Valley is a State of Mind. Not Necessarily a Real Place!" I think that says it all really.

*VOTED FOR BY THE AUTHOR*
*BEST IN AMERICA*
*Tourist Attraction*
*Over The Golden Gate Bridge*
*San Francisco*

Continuing north you hit San Francisco, this is a great city to visit.

I would do all the touristy things including Alcatraz. Watch out for D-Block (the old psych ward) for some reason, can't possible think why! I had a panic attack in here.

When visiting San Fran here are 2 tips; one, take a jacket. Many people get caught because the mist coming off the Bay can make it quite chilly.

Two, if you get chance go over the Golden Gate Bridge with the bonkers retired couple Captain Robert and Co-Captain Marilyn on The Big Red Shiny Mack Fire Engine. Altogether now..."The Big Red Shiny Mack, Fire Engine (ring, ring) The Big Red Shiny Mack, Fire Engine..."

On this trip you put on your fire gear, balaclavas and take in the many sites and districts that make up San Francisco. As if Marilyn wasn't entertaining enough she told us she is in the Guinness Book of Records as one of the few people to have..........what for it........ "tap-danced on top of the south tower of the Golden Gate Bridge". Did I mention they were bonkers!

Ok so having left your heart in San Francisco your next stop will normally be the Napa wine region. You are likely to pass Berkley, the famous Ivy League university. I would give this a miss, apart from the famous University of California (which isn't that nice) there is nothing there.

# Hearst Castle, California

I had a similar experience when I visited Yale in Connecticut a few years later. Apart from the beautiful academic buildings, I'm sorry to report it is a "bit of dump". But I am happy to tell you that Harvard in Massachusetts is quite nice. Admittedly no were near as nice as Cambridge or Durham University, England.

I would however recommend stopping at Point Reyes on the way up. The Point Reyes National Seashore Lighthouse offers dramatic coastal views of the Californian coast to the south. It is particularly dramatic if you go in the winter months. The crashing waves and blustery winds of the North Pacific are exhilarating.

Heading inland to Napa, unsurprisingly you will encounter lush vineyards wine shops and restaurants. I would recommend checking out some of the following events to get the entire Napa experience in one hit.

The Napa Valley Mustard Festival is a red-carpet event normally held during the months of February and March. Here you can enjoy world-class wines, live music, visual arts and auctions. It is well attended and often sells out so book early. www.mustardFestival.org.

Alternatively I would check out the annual Russian River Valley Winegrowers Crab and Fennel festival. Normally held in March at the Sonoma County Fairgrounds in Santa Rosa. These two combined festivals allow you to roll up your shirt sleeves, crack some fresh Dungeness crap and enjoy Russian River Valley wine.

The great food and wine on offer is a treat, but meeting the winemakers and growers is the highlight. As well as the bizarre hermit crab races, I called mine "Kermit the Hermit!"

Finally I would recommend getting a limousine tour so you don't have to drive. It's a unique way to see Napa and the surrounding regions. Or look into the Wine Cruise or Sierra Railroad which I was told were very good.

Although I liked Napa I didn't think it was a patch on the Champagne and Cognac regions of France or Stellenbosch in South Africa. But you should go at least once to say you have been.

Instead my own personal recommendation would be to venture to the Mendocino Wine Region to the north of Hearst Castle instead.

A lot less well-known, this is where the Napa wine people tend to hang out away from the crowds. But strictly speaking the Mendocino Wine Region is not really in one spot on the map, which is also what makes it that little bit special. Generally speaking it would be anywhere North of Santa Rosa heading towards Mendocino itself.

Have a good drive around and look out for small vineyards off the beaten track or stop and ask the wine labourers for suggested tasting spots.

Whilst driving off the beaten track I saw a hare get hit by a car. It had broken hind legs and was suffering, so after putting it to sleep, I put it out of its misery. Poor bugs!

# Hearst Castle, California

Ironically the next town I came across was called Hopland. "Bright Eyes, Burning like Fire..." was looping in my head. So needing a stiff drink after the Bugs Bunny incident I was delighted to find a hotel, wine shop and brewery smack bang in the middle of this one street town.

I enjoyed the famous California beers at the Mendocino Beer Company, namely Eye of the Hawk, Red Tail and many more. I think of myself a bit of a beer expert, having been to a handful of beer festivals most recently in Berlin. I have to say for an American beer it was great.

My next stop off (after booking in the hotel) was the absolutely fabulous wine shop in the heart of Hopland called Sip. A fairly new small business, the owner Bernadette has lived in the area all her life. She knows the region's smaller, more labour intensive wine growers personally.

So her wine shop and tasting room offer some of The Best wines of the region. Not only that, she can tell you a story or two about the origins of the wine. Although alittle pricier you know the wine you are buying has probably not been mass produced and has normally come from a single small harvest and definitely locally sourced.

Leaving Hopland the sequoia filled Mendocino National Forest is a good stop off point to enjoy all the wine you have bought.

From springtime onwards there are events at Lake Mendocino with names like Classic Concerts by The Lake. There's nothing better than a picnic, locally sourced wine, cheese and a cool Californian summer's evening listening to music. And Relax...Welcome to Northern Californian.

I eventually made my way all the way up to Eureka, California before I reminded myself of The Rules of my journey and decided to head back south towards Hearst Castle.

This time I went a completely different way back. That is what is so good about this whole area, you could spend weeks and weeks exploring there is so much see and do. Never mind Route 66 (in my opinion, over-rated) head to the Pacific Coast Highway. Route 101 Rocks, you heard it here first folks!

When I got to Hearst Castle I was surprised at how big it was. Having lived in California I know how expensive real estate is and this place has acres of it. Well 250,000 acres and fourteen miles of prime coastline to be precise.

Weirdly although you may have never heard of it, immediately it's familiar because of the many films and TV shows it has been in. The history behind this magnificent mansion was also fascinating.

Hearst Castle is actually a National Historic Landmark and was designed by a woman architect Julia Morgan between 1919 and 1947 for newspaper magnate William Randolph Hearst.

# Hearst Castle, California

Sadly he never saw it completed because he died in 1951. So in 1957 the Hearst Corporation donated the property to the State of California. One condition of the Hearst Corporation's donation of the estate was that the Hearst family would be allowed to use it when they wished.

Since that time it has been maintained as a State Historic Park, meaning the estate and its considerable collection of art and antiques is open for public tours. Despite its location far from any urban centre, the site attracts roughly one million visitors per year.

Hearst formally named the estate "La Cuesta Encantada" (The Enchanted Hill). But as rich people often do, the family called it something completely understated The Ranch. I must remember one day to call my 18 carat gold toilet not "The Throne", but "The Bog!"

Like any wealthy eccentric, William Hearst kept buying too many nice things for Hearst Castle and Julia Morgan was constantly having to adapt to her owner's persistent design changes. Men!

In the end Hearst Castle featured 56 bedrooms, 61 bathrooms, 19 sitting rooms, 127 acres of gardens. An indoor and outdoor swimming pool, tennis courts, a movie theatre an airfield and the world's largest private zoo. Yes, zebras and other exotic animals still roam around the grounds today.

The Neptune Pool patio features an ancient Roman temple front transported wholesale from Europe and reconstructed at the site. Hearst was an interminable tinkerer and would tear down structures and rebuild them at a whim. Apparently, the Neptune Pool was built and rebuilt three times before Hearst was satisfied.

Invitations to Hearst Castle were highly coveted during its heyday in the 1920s and 30s. The Hollywood and political elite often visited usually flying into the estate's airfield or taking a private Hearst-owned train car from Los Angeles.

Charlie Chaplin, Cary Grant, the Marx Brothers, and Winston Churchill were among Hearst's A-list guests. I bet they were some great parties.

It is sad that Hearst never saw the Castle completed in his lifetime.

But on a positive note for all the "Sisters" out there, Julia Morgan received notable accolades for her accomplishments as designer and civil engineer on the project. "You go Girl, back in the 1920s".

I would highly recommend taking one of the many tours. I did both a day and night tour. Both were excellent and gave you a completely different perspective.

As the Mansion is not air conditioned, going early evening is wise because it is not as humid inside.

# Hearst Castle, California

Once inside you walk around from room to room behind guide rails. With each room seeming to have a different architectural style from art-deco, baroque to gothic across the centuries. For example, one room features a full length wooden 100 seating dinning table within a heavily wooden panelled room. Think Great Hall at Hogwarts, to picture the scene.

In the next room you walk into what feels like a Victorian French boudoir with pastel drapes and floral print furniture. By contrast you walk into another wood panelled room with huge wooden triforium arches which feels like you are inside a medieval church.

I counted at least 100 mirrors room to room before I got bored. In some rooms things are dotted around as if the residents had just left the room, giving it that personal touch.

Eventually you will come out onto one of the many balconies or verandas. Here you get a panoramic view of the Pacific Ocean in the distance.

There is so much to take in, Hearst Castle is over-elaborate in places, almost garish. It wouldn't be out-of-place in a Hollywood movie like Oceans Eleven, The Hangover or Jackass. I think even Nero himself would have been phlegmatic about it.

That could of course just be "my Englishness" coming-out. We do like things to be tasteful after-all. They are called "Stately Homes" for a reason!

So that was Northern California, in the summer it is very pleasant. Hot without being sticky and plenty of events and places to visit. With Hearst Castle definitely on the list.

The scenery on the drive from Southern to Northern California was spectacular with plenty of places to stop off and have a look around. You could easily fill 4-6 weeks with enjoyable activities from golfing, wine tasting, surfing not to mention a quick trip on...altogether now... "The Big Red Shiny Mack, Fire Engine". Like the "It's a Small World" theme at Disney, this never leaves you!

As regards Hearst Castle I think it is was one of those "Love it" or "Hate it" places. Each person will come away with different feelings about it. But there is one thing I can guarantee you. Everyone will certainly wish they owned it!

# IF YOU HAVE MORE TIME ...

## Outdoors People

The Tour of California is the largest cycling event in America, a Tour de France-style road race, it challenges the world's top professional cycling teams. Covering more than 750 miles over nine days through February.

Also in February, Healdsburg holds its annual Wild Steelhead Festival - with the spoils of the fishing competition being served at the buffet dinner held at the Hotel Healdsburg.

For the best surfing in Northern California I would check out the following beaches Bolinas, Carmel and Sand Dollar.

## History, Culture & Gifts

When the Spanish began colonizing California, a key component of the plan was to Christianize the indigenous peoples already inhabiting the land. Under the management of father Junipero Serra, the Spanish built a series of 21 missions from San Diego to San Francisco between 1769-1823. These missions established a safe passage dubbed El Camino Real or The Royal Road. As well as bringing wine making to the region.

Looking for a different gift, check out the exclusive RAS galleries they offer art glass, sculpture and ceramics. As you may expect the uniqueness of their work comes at a price, but worth it. Their gallery can be found in Yountville, California.

## Photographers (People & Places)

For your own personal Great Hall at Hogwarts picture I would organize a private dinner at the Cast Room at Merry Vale. The wooden barrelled wall to ceiling room, lit by candlelight is a unique setting. Why not get yourselves some robes and wands and make the most of it!

For vineyard lovers head to the hills of Garre Winery and Livermore, it offers great shots of wine fields with undulating valleys and red roof-tops.

Head away from Monterey up into the Santa Cruz mountain regions towards Salinas. This is a great scenic highway with the backdrop of mountains and sea-views for that perfect shot.

## Only in America ...

Did you know that California has its own Old Faithful Geyser located in Calistoga. The area around Geyserville, north of San Francisco, has the largest geothermal plants in the world. Today Mount Lassen has active boiling mud pots, hot springs and steam rising from the side of the mountain.

If you are a fan of Zinfandel wines then you will probably enjoy attending the Zinfandel Festival held annually in January normally in San Francisco. There is no other place in the world a wine lover can experience "Everything Zinfandel". It has annual attendance of around 10,000 people with over 273 Zinfandel wineries in attendance. Cheers!

# USA VOTED - TOP 6 'OTHER' LETTER "H" DESTINATIONS ...

## Hollywood, California
Distance from Hollywood to Los Angeles International Airport is 24 miles or approx. 29mins.

## Hershey, Pennsylvania
Distance to Harrisburg International Airport is 11 miles or 20mins.

## Honolulu, Hawaii
Downtown to Honolulu International Airport is 7 miles or 13mins.

## The Hamptons, New York
Distance to LaGuardia Airport is 97 miles or approx. 1hr 55mins.

## Holland, Michigan
Distance to Gerald Ford Airport to is 45 miles or approx. 53mins.

## Hilton Head, South Carolina
Distance to Hilton Head Airport is 4 miles or 9mins.

# *I* is for...... Independence

**Independence, Kansas -** With history & culture, distilleries, golf-ball hail, festivals, rodeos, museum's, tornadoes and the Land of Oz. I thought Kansas was meant to be a dull flatland prairie State with nothing but farmlands!

"I" is for independence, Kansas. I became very familiar with the State of Kansas due to the number of times I seemed to drive through it on my A to Zee journey across America. Unfortunately for me the I-70 became My New Best Friend, miles and miles of flat land prairies, farming and small towns.

I have to admit I never looked forward to driving across it. On one such journey to cheer myself up I bought this T-shirt that said "Cow, field, tractor, farmer. Cow, field, tractor, framer. Cow, field, tractor, farmer. Cow, field, tractor... Yep, you're in Kansas Al' Right!"

Undeterred if you are prepared to do further research, you'll discover that Kansas offers more than just farming pioneer heritage. To prove this and to break up the journey, I used to visit the many breweries, distilleries and saloons ideally dotted the southeast of the state. With Kansan names like High Noon, Little Apple, High Plains and Tall Grass. Not forgetting the state is littered with vibrant big cities and small towns with welcomes as warm as their summers.

So should you ever find yourself on the I-70, my advice would be to come off it from time to time to see Kansas; don't just drive through it, like everyone else. Attend a rodeo, check out its Native American and early settler history. You could "Go to, Then Get Outa' Dodge City!" Not to mention the 24 State Parks, festivals, events and attractions held annually across the Sunflower State.

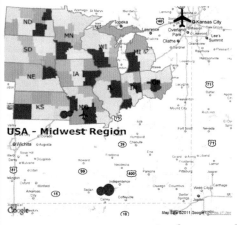

USA - Midwest Region

So Independence, Kansas is in the south east of the State. Not to be mistaken with Independence, Missouri where President Harry S. Truman lived.

I think Independence received so many votes because it is a popular word in American culture.

After all don't forget Independence Hall, Philadelphia and The Declaration of Independence are commonly used phrases throughout an American's childhood. In the same realm as words like Justice, Liberty, Freedom and Democracy.

# Independence, Kansas

However if you asked Americans which State? They generally didn't have a clue but knew "There had to be one somewhere in America". However a handful of people genuinely Voted for Independence, Kansas because of its link with the wholesome television show Little House on the Prairie.

For those of you not familiar with the show it depicts an small early 1800s homestead settlement family. Who worked the land, went to school and attended church every Sunday. Similar to the other wholesome show which came out around at the same time The Waltons.

The book Little House on the Prairie was written by Laura Ingalls Wilder. The Ingalls family–Charles, Caroline and young children Mary, Laura and Carrie–made rural Montgomery County, Kansas their home from 1869 to 1871.

Pioneer families at the time endured many challenges and hardships that came with the untamed territory. It was those events that left an indelible imprint on the mind of young Laura and was the inspiration for her books.

Located 30 miles south-west of Independence the Little House on the Prairie historic site includes a replica one-room cabin located near the original site where Laura Ingalls Wilder lived as a child. It also includes Sunnyside School House that was used from 1872–1947 and an original Post Office School and gift shop.

Visiting this place reminded me a little of why I went to see Southfork Ranch in Dallas, made famous by the 1980s television show of the same name.

That is, if you didn't get engrossed in the fantasy and world in which the television show characters lived, then I wouldn't recommend a visit. Because as you arrive at the site of the Prairie House, it will just look like a random set of buildings in the middle of nowhere!

Just like at the South Fork Ranch in Dallas , it wasn't the house, it was the experience. Seeing The Gun that Shot JR and being surrounded by a coach load of Italians dressed in cowboy shirts, hats and boots that made it so special.

So if like me, you bought into 'the idea' of prairie homestead living and loved the fact that Charles Ingles seemed to cry in every episode!

Then you will be able to reminisce at a by-gone era and instead warm to these random buildings in the middle of nowhere. Imagining poor blind Mary Ingalls having to feel her way around the farm. They don't make em' like that anymore!

Leaving The Little House, heading to Independence itself, there are some notable attractions. Like the William Inge Theatre, Elk City Reservoir and the Independence Science and Technology Centre. But I would suggest this is a town you could easily see in one day, or pass through on the way to somewhere else. Which is travel speak for "it was a bit dull!"

# Independence, Kansas

That is, unless of course you arrive towards the end of October when Neewollah happens. This is a celebration featuring musical carnival shows, concessions and a grand parade attracting more than 80,000 visitors each year. Being Southeast Kansas' largest celebration. There's even a Pie Eating Competition, sign me up!

Clearly I couldn't talk about the state of Kansas and not mention the Wizard of Oz or tornadoes. I did experience my first tornado whilst traveling across Kansas in "Reggie the RV" (you can see pictures at www.atozee.acrossamerica.com).

Being from Blighty this was obviously a brand-new experience for me. I realized quite quickly my reference points regarding "What to do if Caught in a Tornado" would be what I had learnt from the Discovery Channel. Or rely on potential urban myths like "lie in the ditch" or "hide under a bridge" advice from the urban masses.

I knew from watching storm chasers on the Discovery Channel that driving towards the descending black cloud slowly filling the horizon is generally not considered a good idea. Especially in an RV!

But I continued unawares and didn't start to worry until the golf ball hail started to slam down on the RV roof with dull thuds.

Fascinated by my first viewing of golf ball hail, I pulled in at the next junction and managed to park Reggie safely between a Taco Bell and Wal-Mart.

Whilst I was busy taking photographs and trying to catch one of the golf ball hailstones. Honestly, hours of fun!

I failed to notice the storm had got significantly worse with the rain, thunder and lightning bolts becoming more and more ferocious. The entire sky had gone from day to night.

The arrival of the police, who ushered me away from the RV and into to the Wal-Mart entrance made me realize the seriousness of the situation.

So here I am a naïve English girl travelling alone, huddled-up with around 300 Kansans in a Wal-Mart entrance. "Auntie Em, Auntie Em..." was all I could think of.

Although there was still a black sky and rain thundering down. Just as fast as the storm had ridden-up, there was a strange eerie calm.

# *I* is for...... **I**ndependence

There was a twinkle in my eye as I listened to the people around me as they recounted stories of previous tornadoes. But my curiosity and excitement soon retracted when I realized from their stories the destruction tornadoes can have on small town communities in State's like Kansas.

Then to my absolute surprise and shock the sky turned an emerald green, just like the colour of the witch in The Wizard of Oz.

The wind became tremendous and we where ushered away from the glass doors of Wal-Mart by the police.

In the distance you could see several large honeycomb shaped clouds disbursing from the horizontal skyline to the ground below. They seemed huge in diameter moving very fast from right to left across the landscape. The green sky had now been replaced with a bright light, blowing winds and continuous torrential rain.

After about 10 minutes the police radio crackled back into life and seemed to suggest there had been tornado activity in the area. But luckily it had just passed us by.

After a while the Police advised it would be safe for us to proceed to our vehicles in a orderly fashion. With the caveat of staying tuned into local radio stations for further updates.

Travelling in the RV, I decided to hang around for a good half an hour. I got talking to the hospitable locals and got first-hand real life tornado advice, just in case.

You will be happy to know that laying flat in a ditch of a low-lying area is actually sound advice if you are unable to seek any other form of shelter during a tornado.

Not just any old ditch mind, make sure you pick one that is unlikely to incur flash flooding. I mean, if you're going to "go" then I would much rather die spinning around in a tornado funnel than be found drowned in a slowly draining ditch! How embarrassing!

Staying on the Wizard of Oz theme I would recommend a visit to Wamego, Kansas and the Oz Museum. This is home to one of the largest collections of privately owned Wizard of Oz memorabilia in the world.

You will find yourself surrounded by early 1900s MGM artefacts including displays of Dorothy, Tin Man, Scarecrow, the Wicked Witch and Glinda the Good Witch.

I also went to Dorothy's House in Liberal, Kansas but this came in a poor second compared with Oz. If passing by then I would encourage you to pop in, especially if you have small children. There is something quite heart warming about walking on The Yellow Brick Road at Dorothy's house.

So that concluded my first tour of Kansas. Having done my research I enjoyed exploring to see what it had to offer. But like many of its neighbouring states of Oklahoma, Missouri and Iowa it soon became a State I went through rather than stayed at ... Especially the 9th, 10th and 11th...time. Thank you Kansas, it was fun while it lasted!

# IF YOU HAVE MORE TIME ...

## Outdoors People

Kansas has many State Parks, I would recommend Cedar Bluff State Park and WaKeeney. Wakeeney has a stunning lake just off the I-70 in the north west part of Kansas.

Or check out Canton, central Kansas and visit the McPherson Mike and Maxwell Wildlife Refuge which has herds of bison and elk roaming along the byway. At one time there were 800 million Bison in America, now generally managed, there are only around 800,000 left.

You are never too far away from a rodeo in Kansas. Check out the Flint Hill's Rodeo in Strong City, Garden City's Big Rodeo or Dodge City's Roundup Rodeo. Events feature steer roping, barrel racing and other expertly performed feats by cowboys and cowgirls. Yeehar!

## History, Culture & Gifts

Notable civil war locations are Fort Leavenworth, Fort Scott, the Eisenhower Presidential Library and the Museum at Abilene. Nicodemus is a tiny town but highly symbolic to African Americans because it was founded by former slaves after the civil war around 1877.

Kansas also has a strong native American past when tribes ruled the western prairies of the Sunflower State. Wichita's, All Indian Centre chronicles their struggles guarded by The Keeper of The Plains statue on entry. There are also several powwows at the Council Grove attracting 10,000 visitors in June. Medicine Lodge Indian Peace Treaty Pageant in September re-enacts the signing of Treaty in 1867 as well as tribal dancing and a rodeo.

## Photographers (People & Places)

Springtime is RiverFest time which attracts 300,000 people to the parks, pavilions and pathways along Wichita's Arkansas River. This nine-day event packs in a stunning line-up of arts and crafts, family fun activities, sweet sugary treats and races on the river. Love it - there is even a dodge ball competition!

Festival goers can listen to a range of concerts and more than 100 bands both up-and-coming and established local talent. Check out: http://www.wichitariverfest.com

## Only in America.....

Visit Yoder, NW of Wichita. Where the Amish community continues to grow with homely restaurants & shops. Drawing visitors fascinated by their simple lifestyle.

Lindsborg, is affectionately known as Little Sweden. Swedes founded the community in 1869. Today, blue and yellow Swedish colours wave from every lamppost on the main street, lined with unique shops. Continuing this theme Hayes, is known as the German capital of Kansas when the first Russian–Germans arrived in 1876. Today they have their own Deutsche Oktoberfest at the Ellis County Fairgrounds in Sept. Or there is Fort Hays State University, Oktober Fest to sample.

# USA VOTED - TOP 6 'OTHER' LETTER "I" DESTINATIONS ...

**Indianapolis, Indiana**
Distance to Indianapolis International Airport is 13 miles or 25mins.

**Ithaca, New York**
Distance to Syracuse Hancock International Airport is 62 miles or 1 hour.

**Irvine, California**
Distance to John Wayne Airport is 7 miles or approx. 13mins.

**Idaho Falls, Idaho**
Distance Idaho Falls Airport is 4 miles or 13mins.

**Isle of Palms, South Carolina**
Distance to Charleston International Airport is 23 miles or 34mins.

**Iron Mountain, Montana**
Distance to Ford Airport is 38 miles or 10mins.

*J is for......*

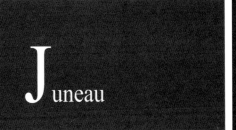

J uneau

**Juneau, Alaska** - One of the most remote, yet dramatic landscapes I visited across the whole United States. Alaska is a truly unique destination and an experience that cannot be matched anywhere else in the World.

"J" is for Juneau, Alaska. Having just completed my journey to Independence, Kansas it looked as though I would be heading to Jackson Hole, Wyoming. Then by chance I met a Sergeant at an airport who was due to be shipped out to Afghanistan that day. As fate would have it, we got talking about my journey. His Vote for Juneau tipped the balance, the next day I found myself driving to Little Rock in Arkansas and jumping on a flight to Seattle and onto Alaska.

The fact that you have to make a concerted effort to get to Alaska means the excitement begins from the minute you get to the airport. Stopping off in Seattle (again!) then flying north you could see the snow-capped peaks of Washington State with Mount Rainer bursting through the clouds. The journey was long, but magical.

It seemed the more remote the place, the smaller the mode of transportation became. The final plane from Ketchikan, Alaska to Juneau only held about 30 people meaning you felt every stick turn made by the pilot.

It was worth it though the journey was breath-taking, after all 17 of the 20 highest peaks in the United States are located in Alaska. So you'll find yourself glued to the window. Based upon the journey alone, I knew Alaska was going to be an amazing experience.

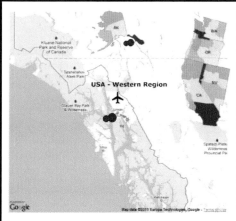

On arrival the taxi driver was astounded to discover I had made no prior accommodation arrangements. I had arrived on the same weekend as the Native American Celebration, so Juneau was full.

So it felt fated once again that a hotel downtown had just had a cancellation minutes before I arrived. I was a little disheartened though to find out my room was in the basement.

But I soon discovered this was a blessing in disguise because the sun was setting at 11pm and rising at 1am. So the basement room provided perfect darkness.

# Juneau, Alaska

On arrival I went to check out Celebration it is a 4-yearly event that brings together all the Native American tribes from the rest of the United States. This was very interesting showcasing the traditions of the differing tribes. With traditional costumes, dancing and foods for you to try. I had Indian Fried Bread which tastes like a mixture of Yorkshire pudding and doughnut. They have it for breakfast covered in jello (jam). Yummy!

To fully appreciate Juneau it is important to get acquainted with the State of Alaska, which like Hawaii, is very different to the other States that make-up America.

Here are some facts, if you superimposed a map of Alaska on the lower 48 States, Alaska would extend from coast to coast. I was told a statistic that if you walked 1 square mile a day across Alaska it would take you around 2,000 years to complete it.

In 1867 the then United States Secretary of State William H. Seward offered Russia $7.2m or 2 cents per acre for Alaska. But officially Alaska only became the 49th state on the 3rd of January 1959.

The term Alaska refers to Alaska's original inhabitants the Aleut, Eskimo and Indian groups. Nearly one-third of Alaska lies within the Arctic Circle and the state boasts the lowest population density in the US.

Oil is the state's most valuable natural resource. The area includes what is thought to be the largest oil field in North America.

This makes Alaska residents eligible for the Permanent Fund Dividend, around $1,000 paid every year simply because they live there. Each person's share of the state's vast oil wealth is met with fanfare and is carried live on TV state-wide from the Governor's Office.

The fishing and seafood industry is the second most prominent employer as most of America's salmon, crab, halibut, and herring come from Alaska.

As if to underline this point, I enjoyed drinks and dinner at The Hanger were I met a young Alaskan native who had lived and travelled across most of the State.

Instead of showing me cute pictures of his buddies, pets or family. He took great pride in showing me pictures on his I-phone of his most recent "kills" including deer, bear, huge cod and wild boar.

I soon came to the conclusion that if Armageddon ever occurs I will somehow get myself to Alaska. Because these people know how to kill and store things to survive in the dramatic terrain and temperatures recorded as low as -80°.

Although Juneau is the capital of Alaska it has a relatively small downtown area that can be easily walked in half a day. You're surrounded by snow topped mountains framing the Juneau Harbour around the Gulf of Alaska.

The view from The Hanger Bar has to be one of the best views from any bar I have been to anywhere in the world.

# Juneau, Alaska

There will inevitably be at least one cruise ship in the harbour. Hundreds pile off, eat some king crab, shop and say "They've been to Alaska" but I would strongly disagree. I stayed in Juneau for 14 days and didn't think that was enough time, there was so much to do.

Unsurprisingly it caters to the cruise tourists and is made up of souvenir shops, provincial museums, bars and restaurants. But as most of the cruise ships have departed by 9pm, this was the best time of the day to go out (in bright day light) and get to know the 'real' inhabitants of Juneau.

If you are lucky enough to spend an extended amount of time here then you will appreciate the warm welcome and hospitality you will receive everywhere you go.

I would recommend the Red Dog Saloon or The Hanger Bar as good starting points. The Red Dog Saloon is great fun, this sawdust floor bar has stuff everywhere. Bits of boat, stuffed animals, messages from around the world, plane bits and underwear. Make sure you take a trip to the toilet as I think this was probably the best comical graffiti I found anywhere in America. My favourite being "Fox News on Sarah Palin—Hair and Unbalanced!"

To underline the "anything goes" atmosphere, instead of handing out pocketbook matches they hand out pocketbook condoms with the words "You Have Got to Be Putting Me On" printed on the back.

I more or less tried every restaurant in town and they were all very good.

Especially the seafood in some of the more ethnic spots like the Indian, Chinese or Japanese.

The only one which I personally didn't care for, was the Borsht dumpling soup shop at the harbour area. I think it was just me though, because it was very popular with the local inhabitants. It was their equivalent of late night/early morning "I have had too much to drink" sustenance before hitting the sack.

My top choices of restaurant both served seafood in completely opposite settings. Firstly, was The Twisted Fish Company (eat early or late and miss the cruisers). Here I had a Nordic style cold platter with smoked fish, capers, compotes and salad.

Secondly, for any Deadliest Catch fans for something quick and less formal you must check out Tracy's King Crab Shack. Always busy, it serves huge King Crab on plastic plates from an outdoor cabin.

# J is for...... Juneau

For those of you that have been fooled by restaurant menus claiming to serve King Crabs, which are really Opillios. Once you eat the "real deal" I guarantee you will never be fooled again. These crab are the size of a small child's knuckle and arm.

I got talking to Tracey and it turned out she was originally from Hertfordshire in England and like many Alaskans somehow found herself coming to visit and just never left!

My other recommendation would be to spend an afternoon at the Alaska Brewing Company.

VOTED FOR BY THE AUTHOR

BEST IN AMERICA

Alaskan King Crab

Tracy's Crab Shack

Juneau

I've found on my trip across America that each state, region or area quite often has specialist beers and Alaska was no different. They offer a range of beers for you to try and buy but unfortunately no international shipping. Boo!

Right next door is Jerry's Meat and Seafood where the Juneau inhabitants get their fresh produce. Unsurprisingly this being Alaska, you can pick up such delicacies as buffalo, moose, smoked fish and some amazing seafood dips.

All the activities you do in Alaska will be "amazing" because the scenery is so perfect. From whale watching, visiting glaciers, hunting, snow-mobiling and fishing. Here are some of my highlights:

Alaska and this whole region is famous as some of the best fishing and hunting in the world.

All the anglers and hunters I met (normally grown men) were as excited a school girls to be here. They were busy hiring boats, planes, helicopters and snow mobiles to find the most remote spots.

For more information check out the hotels leaflets and guidebooks. Were you'll find numerous chartered excursions for the novice.

Even with my limited knowledge and having tasted the local food, you begin to appreciate the pristine and natural environment you are in. So hunting in it must be special.

My next highlight would be the Tracy Arm and Sawyer Glacier Cruise. This was a meandering water cruise taking in the area's wildlife, glaciers and waterfalls. Concluding at the Tracy Arm Glacier itself.

After a 2 hour journey through iceberg filled waters and wildlife round every corner eventually you arrive at The Tracy Arm Glacier. It is a 60ft solid wall of bluey/white crumbling ice.

In the relative silence we waited whilst the glacier creaked, cracked and then tumbled into the freezing water. Making the boat sway violently as a mini wave rippled out across the ocean. Surrounded by this ice world felt like being at Superman's home or in a scene from the ice world in Narnia. It was breath taking.

Thinking about my journey across America I have travelled on some unusual forms of transport like helicopters, hot air balloon, snowmobiles, school bus, donkey (etc). But this was a first, I was stepping into a water plane to fly up into the mountains towards Admiralty Island to see in the wild the Pack Creek Bears.

Trying not to fall in the ice cold water whilst getting in the 4-seater plane can be a bit of a challenge. Then taking off and landing on water was a bit strange, watching the water wash-by as you pick-up speed. If you're scared of flying, this one might not be for you.

# Juneau, Alaska

On arrival you have the sense of how "small" you are when faced with a landscape like Admiralty Island. The water was so clean and clear you could see 10 feet right through it to the bottom containing thousands of mussels and scallops glistening in the sun.

We were met by three Park Rangers, who unbelievably spend their summers isolated out here. I took note that one of them was holding a loaded rifle.

We hiked some distance to a viewing point and the rangers set up a pair of telescopic binoculars so we could view the brown bears from afar.

It wasn't long until we saw the mother bear and her two small cubs. I had seen bears in the wild before at Yellowstone and Maryland. But the isolation of this experience meant it felt much more primitive and exclusive.

It turned out that the telescopic lens was unnecessary, because the male brown bear wanted to enjoy a more exclusive and up-close look at us "humans". He slowly but surely made his way closer and closer, taking an undulating path through deep grass.

It wasn't until the Ranger cocked the rifle that I became a little nervous! Luckily, we all stood perfectly still (as previously instructed) and when the bear came within 15 feet of us the Park Rangers stepped forward and started shouting stern commands.

After staring us down, for what seemed like an age, the bear decided to retreat. Flippin' heck, having been diagnosed with PTSD I generally "don't do fear" anymore, but even that had got my heart racing just alittle!

What an amazing experience, I would advise checking out the work of this man, Stan Prince who spent his life studying the bears in this region.

My final Juneau recommendation would be to take a trip with Era Helicopters and go dog sledding high up on a mountain glacier -- or "Go Mush" as they call it.

Find your Best James Bond sunglasses because flying in a helicopter and landing on a glacier is totally cool. It honestly felt like I was in a Hollywood blockbuster.

# *J is for......* Juneau

On arrival at base camp you will be greeted by over 100 professional huskies and mushers who live and work there during the vacation season and race in the winter.

After meeting the dogs and a safety briefing you are sat or stood on a sled being pulled along at speed through this winter wonderland.

If you think Disneyland is magical then this experience will "blow-you away" and something you will never forget.

The final thing I will say about committing to trips or activities. If you have arrived on a cruise ship or are short of time I would avoid doing whale watching. Unsurprisingly the boats can't get too close so you don't get to see much.

So that was my taster of Alaska, although Juneau was alittle touristy it was a good introduction to the State. It is a great place to have as your base to take trips and explore Alaska further.

Like Hawaii, it really doesn't feel like you are in America when you visit Alaska. It really is a unique State, its remoteness makes it alittle bit backwards compared to the rest of the US. It feels as though they "Make the Rules Up" as they go along. It is about survival, the environment and looking out for each other in Alaska.

If you like hunting and fishing then you must, must, must come to Alaska. The landscape is so unique that before you have cracked open your equipment you will have been through an adventure trying to get to the perfect spot.

Many people on my trip across all 50 States quite often asked me the this question "What was your favourite place?" Alaska and Juneau would most definitely be in My Top 5 favourite destinations.

There are so many adjectives one could use to describe Alaska. So instead you should go and experience it for yourself.

This truly was a trip of a lifetime.

# IF YOU HAVE MORE TIME ...

## Outdoors People

Alaska is an absolute fisherman's mecca, so you must go fishing everywhere and anywhere you can, the more remote the better. But make sure you get professional help, as this is not the terrain you want to get stuck in.

King salmon have been known to frequently weigh up to 100 ponds. The king salmon is also known as the Chinook Salmon and is a popular sport fish. It became the State fish in 1962.

To see Juneau from above take the Mt. Roberts Tram, from sea level to the mid-point is a 1,800 foot elevation that provides sweeping views of downtown and the Gastineau Channel.

## History, Culture & Gifts

Juneau residents have just recently (June 2010) had the chance to take part in the Juneau Farmers Market connecting area producers and consumers.

Anyone who knows me, knows that despite being a girl "shoes" do not feature predominantly in my life. However, I did come across a really unusual shoe shop called Shoefly & Hudsons. Unusual in the respect that they cater for the terrain and the predominant environment in which they operate. By this I don't mean hiking boots, but 'cool' and 'different' winter wellingtons, boots and shoes. To their delight and my surprise I found myself by buying about 5 pairs all at once, which never happens! www.shoeflyalaska.com

## Photographers (People & Places)

I came across a young photographer with a wonderful name Daniel Buckscott. Located in the Wharf Mall on the harbourside he has been lucky enough to photograph Alaska most of his life. I would certainly give him a visit for a unique souvenir. www.WildernessPeaks.com.

The first arrival of white people to Alaska started in the 1740s with Russian fur traders, from turbulent beginnings which spanned 100 years of enslavement, resource depletion and cultural change. For the best example of that I would visit Sitka west of Juneau, which still preserves the Russian legacy of Alaska. A story of war and cultural blending between two superpowers throughout the 1800s. People who know the Arctic say that in the winter you can still walk to Siberia from Alaska. Think I'll pass!

## Only in America.....

One of those weird laws that hasn't been removed from statute books of Juneau is this one : "Owners of flamingos may not let their pet into barber shops!"

One of the largest bears ever recorded in Alaska was a Kodiak Bear; weighing 1,400 pounds and stood 11 feet tall.

The State Flower is the Forget-me-Not, because the plant grows well in most of Alaska's varied climate.

Alaska has one of the largest deposit of jade in the world, including an big mountain full of it on the Seward Peninsula.

# USA VOTED - TOP 6 'OTHER' LETTER "J" DESTINATIONS ...

### Jackson Hole, Wyoming
Distance to Salt Lake City International Airport is 279 miles or 5hrs.

### Jackson, Mississippi
Distance to Jackson Evers Internal Airport is 11 miles or 23mins.

### Jamestown, Virginia
Distance to Hector Williamsburg Jamestown Airport is 10 miles or 24mins.

### Jacksonville, Florida
Distance to Jacksonville International Airport is 14 miles or 22mins.

### Jekyll Island, Georgia
Distance to Jekyll Island Airport is 1 mile or 2mins.

### Joshua Tree, California
Distance to Palm Springs International Airport is 40 miles or 50mins.

*K is for......* **K**auai

**Kauai, Hawaii** - The oldest of the major Hawaiian Islands Kauai is known as the Garden Island with 500 square miles of pristine valleys, magnificent canyons soaring peaks and grandiose waterfalls. Welcome to Paradise.

"K" is for Kauai, Hawaii. The journey from Alaska back to mainland USA, then onto Hawaii was full of stark contrasts. In Alaska I had been piling on the layers in the snowy landscape to then find myself peeling them off in the tropical paradise that is Hawaii and Kauai.

Strictly speaking Kauai is an Island/Country, so I was certainly bending The Rules a little coming here. But it was such a clear winner in the Voting stakes by America I couldn't resist the chance of going to Hawaii for the first time.

I received many Votes for places in Hawaii on all the respected Islands but most people seem to agree that Kauai was the least commercialized and the most Hawaiian. Known as the Garden Island it is 549 square miles of pristine valleys, magnificent canyons soaring peaks and grandiose waterfalls. Welcome to Paradise.

Kauai is the oldest of the major Hawaiian Islands thought to have evolved over 5 million years ago. First inhabitants of Kauai were called the Menehune. Described as a mythical race of small people who constructed aqueducts, fishponds, heiau (places of worship) and other imposing works of stone in a single night. Although thought to have only stood 3 feet tall, they were strong, skilled labourers with an intensive work ethic. Umpa, lumpa...do be..de..day...!

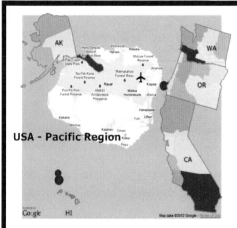

**USA - Pacific Region**

If the Menehune didn't complete a project in one night, it was forever left unfinished.

It was the intrepid explorer Captain James Cook who spotted the island on January 18, 1778 on a mission to find a north-west passage linking the northern Pacific and Atlantic oceans.

Instead of dropping anchor at the other Islands, he sailed passed and two days later set foot on Hawaiian soil for the first time in Waimea, on the west coast of Kauai.

His journal records that "he was greeted with unrestrained awe and admiration."

# Kauai, Hawaii

Villagers mistakenly thought he was Luno, the God of Peace and Fertility. Cook subsequently returned to Hawaii, but was attacked and killed by the natives on the beach at Kealakekua Bay in Hawaii on 14 February 1779.

There are reports that he was cannibalised, but in reality he was prepared in usual ritual way. His heart was divided between tribal chiefs and eaten. His remains were then returned to his crew and buried at sea.

History refers to Kauai as the Separate Kingdom as it was the only major island in the Hawaiian chain that was not conquered by Kamehameha I. Despite numerous invasions and attacks Kauai's King Kaumuali was firm in his resolve to maintain independence.

After ascending to the throne King Kamehameha II decided to kidnap Kauai's King Kaumuali and forced him to marry his father's first wife. So this strange twist of fate, surrounded by much skullduggery, meant Kauai was finally won and the Hawaiian kingdom united.

On arrival if the island looks strangely familiar it will be because it has featured in well over 60 movies and television shows. Including The Descendants, Jurassic Park, South Pacific, Pirates of the Caribbean and Lost.

As you fly in you will probably see Mount Wai'ale'ale. The centrepiece to a stunning mosaic of meadows, valleys, rainforests and sheer coastal cliffs that define Kauai.

To my absolute delight on arrival I was greeted by islanders with the traditional garland of flowers called a Leis.

A fragrant intertwined necklace made from locally sourced orchids and blossoms and the unforgettable "Aloha" greeting. Leis are given to new arrivals or as a farewell with a kiss as a sign of hospitality.

Watch out for the kissing part, lots of men got flustered and made a mess of it. Which resulted in very grumpy wives for the journey to the hotel!

Try to remember as you leave to toss your Leis into the sea; the custom is meant to symbolize the drifting of the Lei back to the shore. A Hawaiian tradition meaning that "someday you will return back to the islands". Fingers crossed!

The custom of wearing a Leis originated with the indigenous Hawaiians, who wove necklaces of leaves, ferns, dried shells, fruits, beads, or bright feathers for personal adornment. Hawaiians celebrate Lei Day on May 1 each year, symbolizing their tradition of friendliness.

I was staying to the east of the island in Kapa'a. If this is your destination of choice check out the hurricane ravaged hotel as you enter the suburban areas. This was once The Coco Palms Resort famous for Elvis Presley's Blue Hawaii.

# Kauai, Hawaii

The hotel has had a torrid history which has meant it has stayed in a state of disrepair since the 1992 Hurricane Iniki hit. This proved particularly useful for a hurricane scene in the Pirates of the Caribbean movie.

When selecting your hotel I would recommend you double-check to see if you have selected one on the beach. Because of the infamous rip curl and rocky outcrops check whether you will be able to swim in the sea.

Although it may look like a beautiful beachside hotel or resort some people are caught out by price and become disappointed if they come to enjoy the tropical warm waters and find they cannot swim in them.

Kapa'a was a great little place, and easy to walk around during the day and at night with ample taxis. It offered everything you would want in a beach resort. Lots of restaurants and bars, shops, supermarkets and places to book activities all within a short distance from each other.

But I found the hotel concierge normally had the best knowledge, especially if you get local inhabitants. Mine at the Aston was super helpful, booking everything for me and was good at negotiating on price on my behalf.

So on the first night I attended an organized Luau at the Coconut Plantation, Kapa'a. This was a great spectacle showing traditional story telling through dance and stunning visual acts. Including some amazing fire dancers. The Hawaiian food and cocktails were also very welcomed.

As there are limited purple foods in the world, I was delighted to find another one here. Taro Mash and Taro Bread, Taro is commonly used in Hawaii and is like a starchy turnip or sweet potato.

The next few days involved a fishing and scuba diving trip around the coast and a helicopter ride which took me all around the island. All of which were fantastic and I would highly recommend. Doing it this way you got to see areas of the island that are uninhabited and inaccessible.

I took in the spectacular views of the 22 miles of the Na Pali Coast line, rising 3,000 feet above the undulating Pacific which unfold along the Carlisle Isle Trail.

We went past four pristine valleys–Kalalau, Honopu, Awa'awapuhi, and Nu'alolog–all tucked away within the bosom of the cliffs.

# K is for...... Kauai

At sunset you could see the shadows dance across the ridges of Mount Wai'ale' ale. You will also be able to spot the aptly named Twin Beaches at Honopu, one long beach split into two by the undulating wreathed cliffs.

Waimea Canyon is known as the Grand Canyon of the Pacific. From the air the montage of shapes shows off the breath taking textures and colours that change with each movement of the clouds.

For a different perspective of Kauai I would take a trip by boat. From the Ocean you get to see the Island's cooling lava rocks or the Coconut Palms at Ke'e Beach. Sailing up the Wailua River you are treated to a tropical Fern Grotto.

However one of the best trips I took was by land. It was kinda' weird and cool all at the same time. With a taxi firm called Jo and Bella (Bella being a white Scotty dog).

Jo has been on Kauai since the early 60s so was able to give me an insight into "real" life on the island.

She took me up and down the coast to some amazing and beautiful spots where we hung out and chilled in the traditional Hawaii "Hang Loose" way. She told me stories of the islands as it was in the 60s and how it has changed over the years which was a great way to understand Kauai's culture.

First stop was the town of Hanalei which is fringed with tarot patches.

Here we had breakfast and the traditional breakfast in Hawaii called Moco-Loco. It is made many different ways but generally speaking it is rice with some kind of marinated meat served warm with a poached egg which you mix all together. It was yummy!

Jo also told me that Hawaiian's love their Spam, in fact it is their national dish.

Having been brought over as a staple during the Second World War.

They even serve Spam in McDonalds and have a Spam Festival in April. Altogether now Spam, Spam, Spam, Spam, Spam, Spam...!

As well as its taro patches Hanalei is famous because of the celebrities that visit it and many songs have been written about it.

It was famed in the 1960s for being the best place to grow Pot because of the tropical environment. Today there is a sizeable hippie population, many of whom live in trees.

Right on que, as if two reaffirm its "way-out" stature as we were driving through it a long haired, elderly man with a knee length beard appeared on his bike. He had a mahogany tan and was completely naked. "Right On Dude!"

The next stop was Kilauea Lighthouse which is on the National Historic Landmark dating back to 1913. A beautifully maintained lighthouse it gazes over the 200 acre Kilauea Point National wildlife refuge.

This was childishly amusing because there were a number of Red Footed Boobies wandering around. This is a seabird which walks around with bright red legs and webbed feet which wouldn't look out of place on a Paris or Milan catwalk!

For the perfect pristine beaches then you should check out Ha'ena Beach, Anahola and Hanalei Bay which were picture perfect and not very busy.

# Kauai, Hawaii

Alternatively, Anini Beach Country Park and Secret Beach are among the choices for a quiet North Shore escape. Or you can celebrity spot on the Pu'upoa Beach.

I have to say that Hawaii has some of the nicest beaches I think I have ever been to in the world. With tropical weather, warm, clean waters and volcanic mountains as the backdrop. It just like you would expect and more.

But for that pure Kauai experience I would grab some food and just hang out near Hanalei Pier or Lydgate State Park which is a great spot for lunch and watching the world go by. Here all the locals gather on the weekend and enjoy the glorious weather, turquoise water and beautiful beaches.

On the eastern side of the island there were two notable waterfalls. Opaeka Falls and Wailua Falls that could be seen from a lookout across the road. You can also enjoy a dramatic view of Kamokila a traditional Hawaiian Village.

To the south of the island is Po'ipu and Kauai's most popular visitor destination called the Spouting Horn. Described as Kauai's —Old Faithfull —Spouting Horn sucks down an energetic wave then forces the seawater up through a lava tube as high as 50 feet into the air.

This whole area also has some very exclusive and acclaimed restaurants to look out for.

My day with Jo and Bella was drawing to an end now so on the way back we took in the Maluhia Road leading to Koloa Town. It smells amazing because it is a 1-mile shaded tunnel of fragrant eucalyptus trees.

As our last stop Jo and Bella took me to the exclusive St Regis Princeville Resort, officially only for residents. Jo doesn't care about Rules, she is Hawaiian afterall! We watched the sun beams breaking through the clouds. Jo explained Hawaiians describe these as "God's Eye Lashes".

So an amazing day ended with us sat high up on the resort watching the sunset and drinking some sparkly fizz. This day, just like Kauai, was truly memorable.

Having had such a nice time with Jo, the day then suddenly flipped on its head. As we returned back to the car, a women was reversing out of the car park.

To be fair to her, Jo had parked somewhat illegally in the car park knowing the area so well. But this lady was labouring getting out of this space going backwards and forwards, backwards and forwards.

At this point I had jumped back in Jo's taxi, as I heard Jo say "Jesus lady, you need to learn how to drive". With that, there was a screeching of brakes and a small, skinning thirty something girl jumped out of the car and started hurling abuse at Jo.

# Kauai, Hawaii

As you know Jo is a taxi driver in Kauai, so I am sure is used to dealing with the odd drunk and abusive customer. But she must not be bigger than about 5ft tall and what came out of her mouth would have made Father Jack blush.

At this point, knowing my Hulk tendencies due to my PTSD I decided it best if "I stayed in the car". But when the male passenger got out of the car hurling abuse, I felt I should intervene.

At the time I have a bright red Mohawk, exactly for this type of situation. There is nothing like a scary haircut to make people think twice when you are travelling alone as a woman in a foreign land.

When I got out of the car, there was a sudden calm washed over the situation. I said the following words *"I just wanted to let you know, that I have called the Police. This lady is a taxi driver who has lived in Kauai all of her life. Who do you think the Police are going to look favourable on 'you two' out-of-towner's or her a defenceless woman just doing her job? Now get the hell out of here!"* They did. Clearly I hadn't phoned the Police.

Jo hadn't calmed down even by the time she had dropped me off at my hotel thirty minutes later.

I mean, I thought this was Hang Loose Hawaii! I hate to say it, but "Yes, they did have a Californian licence plate." Bloody tourists!

That evening based upon Jo's recommendation I decided to head back to the small town of Po'ipu. I enjoyed dinner at The Beach House which has to have one of "the" best restaurant views in all of the US.

Here I sat enjoying the obligatory Mahi, Mahi facing the palm-tree lined volcanic coastline with the turquoise sea lapping the tropical shore line.

That was Hawaii and Kauai all over, it offers sun-drenched beaches, tropical landscapes and rugged coastline but with a laid-back Hang-Loose culture which makes the whole Island so peaceful.

Just thinking of my time there and all the wonderful experiences I had, makes me glow inside.

# IF YOU HAVE MORE TIME ...

### Outdoors People

Princeville is an 11,000 acre exclusive golf resort and community. It you like star spotting then you should go here for lunch. Golfers should check out the award-winning Jack Nicholas designed course. For me, the 13th hole surrounded by the Kauai lagoons is one of the most beautiful holes I have ever had the pleasure to play at.

For snorkelers Hanalei Bay and Po'ipu is very popular because of its shallow, warm and coral filled waters. Surfers should check out the waves at Kalapaki Beach, which is in front of the Marriott resort and Beach Club.

Hikers should visit Koke'e State Park which has over 4,000 acres of wilderness perfumed with native plants.

### History, Culture & Gifts

Winsome Koloa was the site of the first sugar plantations in Hawaii. Each July Koloa Plantation Days celebrate that distinction with a week-long series of events including a music festival, rodeo, ocean sports competitions and Hawaiian entertainment. Also worth a visit nestled in a growth of palms is Waimea Plantation. Which hides a restored sugar Plantation Cottage dating back to the 1930s.

The twin cascades of Wailua Falls tumble 80 feet (taller than Niagara) into a foliage lined pool. In the past divers would jump from the top of the falls into the pool to prove their courage and prowess. When I got there some people where cliff diving. My PTSD has meant that I have a lack of fear, so I was straight in there. No bombing!

### Photographers (People & Places)

Get yourself to the North as the Island to Ha'ena State Park, the paved road will end so you may need a handheld GPS, I had a local instead! Then start walking towards the Na Pali Coast. On arrival you will come across the rock strewn Ke'e Beach and Kauai's north shore in all its glory. Perfect for a dusk or sunset shot.

Ha'ena Beach, Anahola and Hanalei Bay are also picture perfect and not very busy. Anini Beach Country Park and Secret Beach are among the choices for a quiet North Shore escape.

Finally only accessible by air, take a trip to the gaping gorge known as Waimea Canyon, the waterfall spills out of the canyon eroded by a fault in the earth's crust.

### Only in America.....

Hawaii is the most isolated population center on Earth. It is 2,390 miles from California, 3,850 miles from Japan and 4,900 miles from China. But has the highest life expectancy in the United States. Life expectancy for males is 75, for females is 80 years.

Hawaii is the only U.S. state that grows coffee. Coffee plantations in Hawaii make up 6,200 acres. In 2003, 8.5 million pounds of coffee were produced.

The Hawaiian alphabet consists of only twelve letters. The five vowels are A,E, I, O,U. And the seven consonants are H,K,L,M,N,P,W. Unsurprisingly Countdown doesn't show on Hawaiian TV.

# USA VOTED - TOP 6 'OTHER' LETTER "K" DESTINATIONS ...

**Key West, Florida**
Distance to Key West International Airport is 2 miles or 5mins.

**Key Largo, Florida**
Distance to Port Largo Airport is 4 miles or 8mins.

**Kennedy Space Centre, Florida**
Distance to Orlando International Airport is 50 miles or 1hr 6mins.

**Knoxville, Tennessee**
Distance to Knoxville Airport is 4 miles or 12mins.

**Kentucky Derby, Louisville, Kentucky**
Distance to Louisville International Airport is 3 miles or 9mins.

**Kalamazoo, Michigan**
Distance to Kalamazoo Battle Creek International Airport is 6 miles or 15mins.

# *L* is for...... # Lake _____

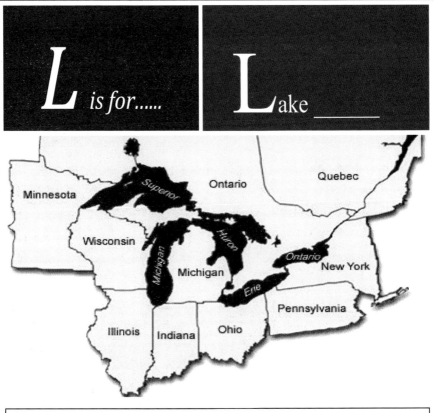

---

**Lake** _____?? - Pick any destination in the United States with the word "Lake" in it and you cannot go far wrong. From Wonder Lake, Moosehead Lake, Fairy Lake, Johnson Lake to Lake Superior. There are so many it is impossible to count them all.

---

"L" is for Lake _____?? One thing I discovered with my trip across America was that if you stayed anywhere near or with the word Lake in it you generally could not go wrong.

There are so many expanses of water in the form of creeks, rivers, ponds and lakes in the USA (named and unnamed) even with today's satellite technology nobody is 100% sure exactly how many there are.

One thing they can be sure of though, is that of the approximately 41 million acres of lakes and reservoirs they are slowly eating into the land mass. A good example of this was after Hurricane Katrina when it was estimated the amount of water gained by the Mississippi River was around 500 square miles.

Minnesota is fondly known as the state of 10,000 Lakes which appears on the license plates. But it is more accurate to say it has over 15,291 lakes. There is a bit of a rivalry with its close neighbour Wisconsin who often claim to have more lakes than they do, but Minnesota wins every time.

But the out and out winner is Alaska, which unbelievably, has over 3 million expanses of water in the State. The two driest States are Hawaii and Delaware.

Being the smallest State, Rhode Island beats them all. With the largest percentage of the State covered by water.

One thing most people seem to be able to agree on though, is that the largest lake is of course the appropriately named Lake Superior in Michigan.

I thought I would have my say and add to the Lake Debate. Having been lucky enough to enjoy a few hundred on my trek across America.

So I will share with you my personal favourites and the reasons why.

# Lake _____, USA

### Lake Lure - North Carolina

Lake Lure covers 720 acres with about twenty -one miles of shoreline. It sits in the heart of Hickory Nut Gorge, carved out by the Rocky Broad River. This crystal clear water flows through a Maltese cross shaped valley to form Lake Lure.

Between the towns of Lake Lure and Bat Cave is Asheville which is the site of the famous Chimney Rock State Park. Nestled in Hickory Nut Gorge, Chimney Rock is a 535-million-year-old monolith rock and is considered one of the most iconic sites in North Carolina.

From its top, you'll soak in the 75-mile panoramic views of Hickory Nut Gorge and Lake Lure. Perched right on the top is the biggest American Flag you will ever see. More affectionally known by Americans as the Stars and Stripes or Old Glory. Honestly this thing was HUGE!

Having stopped at Bat Cave (Kaapow!) for the obligatory photo next to the town sign. I then headed down to Lake Lure.

I stayed at the Lake Lure Inn built in 1927, in the Jennifer Grey suite. The area is famed for being the place where the now iconic Dirty Dancing film was shot.

The thermal lake being used in many of the location scenes including the famous Swayze water lift.

I had a fantastic weekend with an older couple I met from Texas, a wedding party and some of the locals.

The couple I met from Texas must have been in their late 60's, they were sat outside my suite when I checked in. I had gone to get something from Reggie when they got talking to me and I offered them a drink. To be honest they didn't need anymore!

The night progressed and as was often the case (I have one of those faces) their life story had come out.

It turned out they both had mature families and had been together for some time. I was drunkenly told all about their families their children, grandchildren, their life together, how they had met. You get the picture!

After what felt like hours listening to them, I decided I was going to politely excuse myself. When the guy took me aside and asked if he could ask a favour. To my complete surprise he told me he was intending on proposing on this holiday and would I mind recording it on his camera.

He said he was worried about "what she might say". So his plan was to get her sozzled, then ask her. If she said "no", he would blame it on the drink in the morning.

But if she said "yes" he would remind her of it in the morning, gauge her reaction, then ask her properly later that week.

# Lake _____, USA

Firstly I was impressed at his acting, he was sober as a judge, when only minutes earlier he had seemed hammered.

Second, did I really want to be a part of this skulduggery. Hell yeh, Jerry, Jerry, Jerry!

So I duly obliged and in-between the crying and screaming there seemed to be some kind of as "yes" and lots and lots of snogging. Exit Stage left. I never saw them again, I wonder what happened to them next?

I had another strange encounter in Lake Lure this time at lunch in the hotel reception. I got talking to a local Joe who popped in nearly every day to the hotel.

He had been station in England during World War II somewhere on the South coast. He was telling me that during his time there he had been issued with a hand gun.

He had never seen any action, so had never had to use it and had kept it safely stored away all these years.

He explained that he had been cleaning it recently and came across a carefully concealed note inside it. It said "Good luck to the person who gets this and go to it. If ever you get lonely write to: Miss Joyce Thwaites" - followed by her address which was in Essex near the Mills factory.

Apparently many woman who were making weapons at the time would write personal messages.

Stitch them into the holsters as support for the troops on the front-line.

Joe had in fact contacted the Curator at the Imperial War Museum. So fascinated by this piece he asked if he could have it for the museum. Joe agreed and to this day it is on display. Joe has a letter and a picture showing his name and weapon from the museum in London.

Joe has never return back to England due to ill health. So he asked me if I would go and take a look at it for him and maybe send him a picture back and a letter if I did.

I know London like the back of my hand and I have been back many times to see Joe's weapon on display and spoke to the curator.

Of all the places in all the world, I should bump into Joe in lake Lure, North Carolina!

As well as the company what makes Lake Lure so appealing is the fact that you are surrounded by an idyllic green landscape. With the colours of the million dollar water-front homes set against the backdrop of silvery/blue rocks and a bright blue sky.

I was lucky enough to have the company of Mrs Harrington and family who welcomed me on to their boat and vacation house allowing me to enjoy Lake Lure in all its glory.

The Harrington's were made up of a recovering addict rock star from the Grateful Dead and his wife a primary school teacher.

# Lake ____, USA

They were a fantastic couple with small children and incredibly suited. Their whole family made up of super rich stockbrokers and medical professionals.

They were amazingly welcoming allowing me into their lives for the day. Their boat house couldn't have been any closer to the Lake. You could literally jump from the house straight into the Lake.

There wasn't a car in the garage, but a boat. The fire brigade came on a boat not an engine!

If you are looking for a family holiday for all ages, you can't get better much than Lake Lure. I would love to bring my whole family from the UK here one day.

Even more bizarre I also ended-up attending a wedding. It was here the bride introduced me to The Long Island Iced Tea. I had always thought this was some kind of girlie cocktail drink, but Geez-Louise this is like a shot in a tall glass.

Then Jessica behind the bar, soon became everyone's new BFF by introducing us all to the Lake Lure local shot of choice called "Sex with an Alligator". North Carolina being famous for its Alligators!?! You can imagine it all went down-hill from here.

I did wake up though with hundreds and hundreds of Votes. On my arm, my legs, on napkins, scraps of paper, most of which were illegible. How the bride and groom got on their flight that night, goodness only knows?

I also met Shea at Lake Lure who ended-up helping me with the A to Zee project. She was a great help. Thanks Shea.

So that was North Carolina, with fantastically warm and welcoming people and an amazing location. I loved Lake Lure.

### Wilson Lake – Double Head Resort, Alabama

I loved it here too. I stayed in a cabin at the Double Head Resort which sat on the side of Wilson Lake. The resort was fantastic because it offered lakeside amenities as well as many other recreational activities and a pool.

Plus it was "hot, hot, hot" in the South...... whoo-eee!!

I walked from my cabin out to the lake along a gangplank to enjoy the view. Half way down, it felt like it had turned into hot coals so I flung myself into the lake. You could see the steam rising from the souls of my feet. "Jeez, it was like 10am!" I thought to myself.

The States in the south pride themselves on their Southern Hospitality and from my experience it is all true. Not generosity from a materialistic point of view (most don't have much) but from a generosity of spirit.

A sense of devilment with a large slice of fun with the family underpinning everything they do and believe in.

# Lake _____, USA

Of all the Southern States it was in Alabama I enjoyed some real southern hospitality. Once they had got over the Mohawk haircut and I had sworn on the Bible I wasn't a lesbian that is! I'm kidding, but it did feel like that sometimes.

Anyway, at Double Head I spent the 4th of July weekend with a huge group of family and friends all of whom where natives of Alabama through the generations. I think there must have been around 35 in total in the end.

The day started eating and drinking and that pretty much carried on all through the day. With the 100 plus degree heat, when the pool couldn't cool me down I had a disco nap in the afternoon and left them to it.

After a shower and change, I found them all back at the cabin playing Shuffle Board and Horseshoes.

Shuffleboard involves throwing bean bags around 50ft into a hand sized hole on an angled board. Horse shoes is that game you will have seen cowboys play in westerns throwing horse shoes at a stake in the ground.

No cricket or rounder's here I'm afraid, I did mention it, but no-one knew what I was talking about. So I retreated back into my English teacup!

If you know nothing about the American War of Independence and you're English. You need to know this "We Lost" so we generally don't celebrate it.

I did offered to run through the forest wearing a Red Coat whilst the American's chased after me. Fortunately for me, irony and history are pretty much lost on Americans.

So the night wore on with the traditional songs of Star Spangled Banner, Born in the USA and God Bless the U.S.A (etc). All of which I respectfully mouthed through and offered to get the drinks.

One thing I learnt spending so much time in the States is that religion is sure important to them. Especially in the South.

I found out that in the north you are ok saying "God Damn….." but don't diss their mothers. Whereas in the South the opposite is true; you can "Mother…" all over the place, but diss God at your peril. One thing though, "Hell or Not" Alabamians sure do know how to drink. Amen to that!

The night drew to a close with fireworks and even more food and drink. Around 2am there was some kind of a scuffle, when trucks full of men in vests arrived from a nearby town. That was me done.

I thanked them for their Southern hospitality Alabamian style and a fantastic 4th of July. Swapped details (which I duly lost) and hit the hay. Sweet Alabama.

### Lake Erie – New York State

Lake Erie is the fourth largest lake of the five Great Lakes in North America, and the thirteenth largest globally. Bounded on the north by the Canadian province of Ontario.

# Lake ____, USA

To the south the U.S. states Ohio, Pennsylvania and New York and on the west by the state of Michigan. It is in fact this Lake that eventually flows into the Niagara River through the rapids to Niagara Falls.

I found it was an excellent Lake to follow when going from State to State because there was always somewhere nice to stay and it made the journey slightly more interesting. Again anywhere near Lake Erie like Vermillion or Sandusky, Ohio or Erie itself are all great stop off areas for Niagara Falls and considerably cheaper.

My only recommendation would be to make sure you go to Lake Erie first before seeing Michigan and Superior because to do them the other way round takes the "Wow" factor out of the smaller lakes.

### Du Lac- Lake Charles – Louisiana

I arrived in Louisiana just as summer was approaching so the heat and humidity was intense. You longed for any cooling pools of water.

Luckily for me the City of Lake Charles is located on Lake Charles, Prien Lake and the Calcasieu River and is better known as the Lake Area.

Having been to Mardi Gras in New Orleans it was good to find out that "real" Louisianan's come here for their fun. With well over 75 festivals held annually. In fact Lake Charles is referred to as the Festival Capital of Louisiana.

I met some college students who were attending McNeese State University. They told me they had a bayou that ran through the campus grounds called the Contraband Bayou. I didn't believe them at the time but having researched the book, I found out it was true. They were right "students know everything!"

We actually ended-up in L'Auberge du Lac Casino Resort, the less said about that the better. "What Happens in Louisiana, Stays In Louisiana!" I have to say that Louisianans too can drink, sweat, drink, sweat and drink some more! I love the South.

I actually came down to Lake Charles and many other areas of the Gulf Coast (like Pensacola, Mobile Bay, Gulfport) to volunteer after the tragic British Petroleum oil spill.

Wandering onto a beach to volunteer, it wasn't until the Sherriff came over and told me to leave that I noticed it was full of men in orange jumps suits. My Bad, wrong beach!

# *L* *is for......*

# L*ake*____

Mostly my help wasn't needed, so I made a point of eating as much seafood as I could everywhere and anywhere in these BP stricken regions.

That is one thing I will say about Louisiana, damn the food was outstanding everywhere I went. From small hole-in-the wall vendors to fine dining restaurants.

**VOTED FOR BY THE AUTHOR**

**BEST IN AMERICA**

*Weird and Wonderful Food*

*The State of Louisiana*

They sure know how to cook weird and wonderful foods from alligator, grits to hush puppies to fried green tomatoes.

If you consider yourself a foodie, then Louisiana should definitely be on your list of world food cuisine's. If I lived there, I would be the size of a house, not just a bungalow, but the White House. Amazing soul food!

### Lake Tahoe – California

Set in the Sierra Nevada mountain range bordering California and Nevada, Lake Tahoe is the largest alpine lake in North America.

For skiers and boarders this is definitely the place to be in the winter, I counted at least 12 ski-resorts. But Tahoe also offers great water sports from Spring to Fall.

There is also something quite weird about flying from sun-drenched Santa Monica to find yourself 6,000ft up and surrounded by snow only a few hours later.

I enjoyed some boarding in Lake Tahoe, the views at the top of a snow filled mountains are spectacular.

The apres-ski can be alittle pretentious but there is lots of choice and the food and service are excellent.

### Finger Lakes - New York

So named because of their shape, when looking at them on a map the Finger Lakes spread 100 miles from the west near Conesus Lake. Right across the state to the east as far as Otisco Lake.

There are a total of eleven lakes in the Finger Lakes Region. I think it is New York's best kept secret, because you can be at one of the Lakes from downtown Manhattan in less than 4 hours. Even better, it has a really handy airport called the Fingerlakes Regional airport.

Each finger-shaped Lake offers a slightly different set of views and activities to do in the local area.

My personal favourite was Geneva, New York State. Here you can laze along side the lake enjoying some of the regions famous wines. "Yes, New York is famous for its wines." I would certainly take a wine tour if you can.

The sunrise over Lake Geneva is something worth waking-up for. It is also a great stop-off on the way to Niagara Falls. This was the best website I found for more information: http://www.fingerlakes.org

### Deep Creek Lake – Maryland

With my tour of America taking me backwards and forwards coast to coast I experienced Deep Creek Lake at various times during the year. The contrast could not have been any different. In the summer the whole area was teeming with activity, with hundreds of people messing about on the lake. Harley's and bikers everywhere in busy bars and restaurants.

Then when I returned in the winter the entire lake was frozen solid with a good thick layer of snow all around. The bustling streets had been replaced by a sleepy silence. In fact I drove straight across the bridge and didn't give it a second glance.

# Lake _____, USA

It wasn't until I saw a small sign saying Deep Creek Lake, I actually knew I was at the same place.

### Lake Michigan and Lake Superior - Michigan

Lake Michigan is one of the five Great Lakes and is the only one located entirely within the United States.

Lake Superior is the largest of the five traditionally demarcated Great Lakes of North America. As if to underline its huge size the Lake is bounded to the north by the Canadian province of Ontario and the U.S. States of Minnesota, Wisconsin and Michigan.

I grouped these Lakes together because for me they were very similar in terms of how they looked. At the water's edge you cannot see the end of the Lake as it dips over the horizon. So for all intents and purposes if you didn't know better you may have thought it is was an ocean.

The view of Lake Michigan from the north is very different to the view you get from the south. Traverse City (to my amusement pronounced Travor) is a holiday destination on the mouth of Lake Michigan. This area is also famed as being the Cherry Capital of America.

If you are in the area I would recommend a visit to downtown Traverse City. I particularly liked the Traverse City Brewing Company.

You must try the Cherry Heritage Lager with the cherry filled Plevalean Burger sold here. I think it is here that I had The Best French onion soup in America, described as Oatmeal Stout French Onion Soup with grated Swiss cheese. It was boiling and delicious and perfect as temperatures in Michigan can reach as low as –18 and snow as high as 10 ft.

Being the largest producer of tart cherries in the US, make sure you buy something cherry related from Cherry Republic on Main Street. Or come in July when the city holds a week-long Cherry Festival, attracting approximately 500,000 visitors annually.

I made some new friends in Traverse City, one called Cathy. She gave me a Vote for a secretive place called Paradise Cove.

She suggested the place had some kind of magical powers, because when she visits her watch and cell phone stop working.

On her recommendation I made the effort to find the exact location and then took the half mile woodland trek to the Cove. An opening appears through the forest and you encounter the blue waters and high coastal view.

I can confirm it is pretty magical, Cathy was correct the place had a spooky feel about it. It reminded somewhat of the vortex areas I visited later on my trip in Sedona, Arizona.

# Lake ____, USA

I know you're wondering, "No, my watch or mobile didn't stop working." My nose did start bleeding though. (I'm kidding!).

Leaving Lake Michigan to Lake Superior there is plenty to do. There are 6 National Forests and Parks near its banks, so you can imagine the scenery in the whole area is outstanding.

When you get there you will see it lives up to its "Superior" name. The lake could cover the entire land mass of North and South America combined in 1 foot of water. The shoreline alone could stretch end-to-end from the east to west coasts.

Having seen the Lake from all sides, my recommendation would be to see it from the Minnesota side. Specifically I would go to the Lake Superior National Forest near Grand Marais or Big Bay State Park. Here you can enjoy camping right on the side of the lake.

If you are planning on spending an extended period of time here then water sports, fishing and boating are all popular. You could easily entertain yourself in this whole area for a few weeks.

One thing though I wouldn't advise doing though is jumping in Lake Superior because of its depth its freezing.

Away from the water I would also check out the Great Lakes Shipwreck Museum. It was founded in 1978 by a group of divers for the exploration of historic shipwrecks in eastern Lake Superior.

Here you can see preserved artifacts from shipwrecks and understand the vital role the Great Lakes have played in growth of the United States. Remembering the many lives that have been lost while navigating them.

So "L" was for Lakes, which one you decide to go to will be up to you. I visited hundreds during my time in America enjoying them all.

I found it was a really good way to meet the local people, who generally went to the lake near them throughout the year. It seems Lakes and North America go together like Burger and Fries.

So if you get the opportunity, try to see as many as you can. Whether they be local, regional or the larger more famous ones. I guarantee they will all offer good facilities and plenty to do.

# IF YOU HAVE MORE TIME ...

## Outdoors People

You cannot beat hiking at Thompson Lake, Maine or Big Bear, CA in the summer where the scenery and temperatures are just right. Or Ski-ing at Lake Tahoe in the winter.

For some good camping and RV locations with hiking, fishing and the like I would recommend: Copan Lake, Oklahoma, Lake Carlos, Minnesota, Clearwater, Idaho, Lake Martin, Louisiana and the Caddo Lake, Texas to name but a few.

For the water sport enthusiasts, I came across the 55 ft tall beehive shaped rock filled with warm tropical waters at Homestead Crater if you fancy a bit of scuba diving. For some of the best kayaking spots I would head along Route 90 in Montana or The Green River into Lake Powell, Utah.

If you just wanna' enjoy the water and party then I would head to Lake Havasu, Arizona or Key West, Panama City and South Beach all in Florida.

## History, Culture & Gifts

The Great Lakes area gets my vote here as there are quite a few museums which are worth a visit as well as numerous National Parks.

The first inhabitants of the Great Lakes basin arrived about 10,000 years ago. Having crossed the land bridge from Asia or perhaps from South America or the Pacific Ocean. Descendants of the first settlers were using copper from the south shore of Lake Superior and had established hunting and fishing communities throughout the Great Lakes basin. The native people occupied widely scattered villages, growing staples and tobacco.

Crater Lake in Oregon has the clearest water of any lake in the world. At 594m it is fed solely by falling rain and snow, with no inflow or outflow at the surface.

## Photographers (People & Places)

For dark and moody swamp photos I would head to Lake Drummond, Virginia, Everglades, Florida, Bald Cypress Swamp, Illinois.

For some fantastic lake and scenery shots, I would head to the Glacier National Park, Montana, Lake Placid, NY State, Lake Chelan, Washington, Jackson Lake, Wyoming and Mirror Lake, Alaska.

For waterfalls, ignoring the famous ones, my favourites where; Fulmer Falls, Pennsylvania, Multnomah Falls, Oregon, Upper Whitewater Falls, North Carolina, Akaka Falls Hawaii. The Burgess Falls, Tennessee, Sawtooth Wilderness, Idaho, Cathedral Falls, West Virgina. The Mount Rainer National Park Falls, Washington, The Cumberland Falls, Kentucky, Langfield Falls at the Gifford Pinchot National Forest Washington and not forgetting the beautiful Wailua Falls in Kauai.

## Only in America.....

The Great Lakes shoreline is equal to almost 44 percent of the circumference of the earth. If you took all the water out of them, built a swimming pool in the shape of the US it would be 10ft deep. The Great Lakes provides 95% of the fresh water supply for the US.

The state of Michigan is second to the state of Alaska in shoreline miles. Michigan has the longest fresh water shoreline in the world.

Char-gogga-gogg-manchaugg-agogg-chabuna-gonga-maugg is the name of a lake in New England which is more commonly known as Lake Webster. The name means "You fish on your side, I fish on mine. Nobody fishes in the middle". Sensible those Native Americans!

# USA VOTED - TOP 6 'OTHER' LETTER "L" DESTINATIONS ...

### Long Island New York
Distance to La Guardia Airport is 12 miles or approx. 22mins.

### Lincoln Memorial, Washington DC
Distance to Ronald Reagan Washington National Airport is 6 miles or approx. 12mins.

### Lafayette, Louisiana
Distance to Lafayette Regional Airport is 3 miles or 8mins.

### Long Beach, California
Distance to Long Beach Municipal Airport is 3 miles or 9mins.

### Lexington, Kentucky
Distance to Blue Grass Airport is 7 miles or 16mins.

### Lookout Mountain, Tennessee
Distance to Chattanooga Airport is 15 miles or 34mins.

# *M* *is for......* **M**artha & Mac

**Martha's Vineyard and Mackinac Island, Massachusetts & Michigan** - Both summer destinations are unlike anywhere else in the US. On arrival it is like stepping back in time to a Victorian era.

"M" is for Martha's Vineyard and Mackinac Island both of which got exactly the same amount of Votes, I was lucky enough to visit both. I will start with the bigger of the two Martha.

Martha's Vineyard like its close neighbour Nantucket is an island off the south coast of Cape Cod in New England in the State of Massachusetts. To be honest, I have always found this geography quite complicated so here is My Dummies Guide to New England.

Massachusetts is one big state in the north east of America, it has lots of little places with English sounding names like Norfolk, Lincoln, Chelmsford; hence New England. Then the funny curled up toe bit on the coast of Massachusetts is known as Cape Cod. Both Cape Cod and New England are regions inside Massachusetts. Martha's Vineyard is an island just south of them and is only accessible via some kind of island transportation. Which I would advise you *must* book in advance to avoid disappointment.

The island is primarily known as a summer colony often for the rich and famous including Presidents. So unsurprisingly the cost of living on the island is 60 per cent higher and housing prices are 96 per cent higher than the national average. The estimated year-round population is 15,000 residents, however the summer population can swell to over 75,000 people. With around 56% of the Vineyard's homes only being occupied in the summer. Good to know if you are a burglar!

I'm sure like me, you may have heard of Martha's Vineyard but are not really sure why? In fact despite its name, Martha's Vineyard is not a major wine producer. But instead it has been home to Presidents, artists and musicians for decades.

Or arrival it will be strangely familiar, possibly because it has been the location for many famous films. Steven Spielberg filmed the Jaws films here, many of the island natives appear in the film as extras. In June 2005 the island celebrated the 30th anniversary of the Jaws films with a weekend-long Jaws Fest.

# Martha & Mac, MA & MI

Presidents have long been associated with the Island. The Clintons, President Grant and most recently the Obamas have all vacationed here.

But I think it is the Kennedy's for which it has most notoriety. The Kennedy's had a family home here and Jacqueline Kennedy Onassis maintained a home in Aquinnah on the Island until her death in 1994.

The Kennedy's also had the two unfortunate incidents that occurred on the island. The Chappaquiddick incident, as it became known, in 1969 involved Mary Jo Kopechne. She was one of the senators secretarial staff who was killed in a car driven off the Dike Bridge by U.S. Senator Edward 'Ted' Kennedy.

Then in 1999, a small plane crashed off the coast claiming the lives of pilot John F. Kennedy, Jr., his wife Carolyn Bessette and her sister Lauren Bessette.

The "Kennedy Curse" has come to describe the way in which many members of the Kennedy family have tragically died from unnatural or unfortunate causes. Of the 9 Kennedy siblings, 7 have died from tragic causes. Moreover, many of the children of the Kennedy siblings have also died because of tragic causes. Poor family.

There are many famous artists and musicians who are also associated with the area. After his drug overdose in 1982 John Belushi's family chose Abel's Hill Cemetery as his final resting place as he often visited the Vineyard with his family.

The gravestone says "Though I may be Gone, Rock 'n' Roll lives on."

Edward Hopper prevalent in the mid 1900s, painted many nautical scenes in the region and often visited Martha's Vineyard. But despite its rock 'n' roll and modern appeal the island does have an interesting history.

For almost two centuries it had a high rate of hereditary deafness. Having thought to have originated from ancestry in Kent, England. By the late 19th century, 1 in 155 people on the Vineyard was born deaf. Almost 20 times the national average.

Martha's Vineyard Sign Language (MVSL) was commonly used by both hearing and deaf residents until the middle of the 20th century. With marriages between deaf and hearing spouses comprising 65% of marriages on the island in the late 19th century.

# M *is for......* Martha & Mac

**Martha's Vineyard and Mackinac Island, Massachusetts & Michigan** - Both summer destinations are unlike anywhere else in the US. On arrival it is like stepping back in time to a Victorian era.

"M" is for Martha's Vineyard and Mackinac Island both of which got exactly the same amount of Votes, I was lucky enough to visit both. I will start with the bigger of the two Martha.

Martha's Vineyard like its close neighbour Nantucket is an island off the south coast of Cape Cod in New England in the State of Massachusetts. To be honest, I have always found this geography quite complicated so here is My Dummies Guide to New England.

Massachusetts is one big state in the north east of America, it has lots of little places with English sounding names like Norfolk, Lincoln, Chelmsford; hence New England. Then the funny curled up toe bit on the coast of Massachusetts is known as Cape Cod. Both Cape Cod and New England are regions inside Massachusetts. Martha's Vineyard is an island just south of them and is only accessible via some kind of island transportation. Which I would advise you *must* book in advance to avoid disappointment.

The island is primarily known as a summer colony often for the rich and famous including Presidents. So unsurprisingly the cost of living on the island is 60 per cent higher and housing prices are 96 per cent higher than the national average. The estimated year-round population is 15,000 residents, however the summer population can swell to over 75,000 people. With around 56% of the Vineyard's homes only being occupied in the summer. Good to know if you are a burglar!

I'm sure like me, you may have heard of Martha's Vineyard but are not really sure why? In fact despite its name, Martha's Vineyard is not a major wine producer. But instead it has been home to Presidents, artists and musicians for decades.

Or arrival it will be strangely familiar, possibly because it has been the location for many famous films. Steven Spielberg filmed the Jaws films here, many of the island natives appear in the film as extras. In June 2005 the island celebrated the 30th anniversary of the Jaws films with a weekend-long Jaws Fest.

# Martha & Mac, MA & MI

Presidents have long been associated with the Island. The Clintons, President Grant and most recently the Obamas have all vacationed here.

But I think it is the Kennedy's for which it has most notoriety. The Kennedy's had a family home here and Jacqueline Kennedy Onassis maintained a home in Aquinnah on the Island until her death in 1994.

The Kennedy's also had the two unfortunate incidents that occurred on the island. The Chappaquiddick incident, as it became known, in 1969 involved Mary Jo Kopechne. She was one of the senators secretarial staff who was killed in a car driven off the Dike Bridge by U.S. Senator Edward 'Ted' Kennedy.

Then in 1999, a small plane crashed off the coast claiming the lives of pilot John F. Kennedy, Jr., his wife Carolyn Bessette and her sister Lauren Bessette.

The "Kennedy Curse" has come to describe the way in which many members of the Kennedy family have tragically died from unnatural or unfortunate causes. Of the 9 Kennedy siblings, 7 have died from tragic causes. Moreover, many of the children of the Kennedy siblings have also died because of tragic causes. Poor family.

There are many famous artists and musicians who are also associated with the area. After his drug overdose in 1982 John Belushi's family chose Abel's Hill Cemetery as his final resting place as he often visited the Vineyard with his family.

The gravestone says "Though I may be Gone, Rock 'n' Roll lives on."

Edward Hopper prevalent in the mid 1900s, painted many nautical scenes in the region and often visited Martha's Vineyard. But despite its rock 'n' roll and modern appeal the island does have an interesting history.

For almost two centuries it had a high rate of hereditary deafness. Having thought to have originated from ancestry in Kent, England. By the late 19th century, 1 in 155 people on the Vineyard was born deaf. Almost 20 times the national average.

Martha's Vineyard Sign Language (MVSL) was commonly used by both hearing and deaf residents until the middle of the 20th century. With marriages between deaf and hearing spouses comprising 65% of marriages on the island in the late 19th century.

I stayed in Martha's for about two weeks having arrived by ferry. I took in every aspect of the island north, south, east and west.

The main areas of activity being Menemsha where you catch the ferry, Aquinnah and Tisbury.

If you haven't pre-booked a car before arriving then you will have to rely on the buses, motorcycle or bike. The bus service I found (with your bike) to be quite an experience because you could pop on and off when you wanted and it took you around the whole Island. There are well over 26 miles of bike trails to enjoy.

# Martha & Mac, MA & MI

The only risk was knowing when the buses would arrive, so remember to grab a bus timetable when you get off the ferry. Or a few taxi service numbers in case you get completely lost.

The thing that makes Martha's vineyard different to Mackinac Island is that you have to put the effort in to make the most of your visit. On the face of it you could be put off by the expensive houses, pricey restaurants and elitism.

But you would be missing out on what makes Martha's Vineyard a unique Island destination. For example there is a full calendar of events from August right through to the first week in November.

Here are some of my recommendations from my stay:

For an historical perspective I would take a wander around Edgartown whose first English settlers arrived on the Vineyard in 1642. Known as the Great Harbour because of the 19th century whaling industry, you can visit the stately mansions that still grace Edgartown streets today. I would visit Capt Pease's House, Daniel Fisher's House and Vincent's House. The Martha's Vineyard Museum is also worth a quick look.

In the Fall months striped bass, bluefish, bonito and false albacore provide exciting fishing action.

For food and to experience something alittle special, take a water taxi from the harbour side to Lure Grill.

The Harbourside is also where you get the Chappy Ferry, a two minute run across the channel to Chappaquiddick. Before jumping on the ferry check out the brick wall bearing the names of old injured whalers.

Chappaquiddick (or Chappy as the locals call it) is a an island of upland woods, coastal heath, protected bays, and barrier beaches. So perfect for hikers, sea anglers and bird watching.

Also worth a visit is Old Bluffs, it reminded me of the picture postcard places I visited along the Hamptons, Cape Cod and Maine.

It is commonly thought that Americans "don't do irony" so it was funny to come across an American Civil War statue dedicated to Massachusetts (a Union State) by the Confederates!

But that is kinda' the point about Oak Bluffs, it thrives on contradiction and being a bit quirky.

 *M is for......*

 Martha & Mac

It has had a bit of a Hippie reputation beginning nearly two centuries ago when Oak Bluffs flourished as a emerging liberalist spot with people living in campgrounds.

Now the tents have now been replaced with small distinctive cottages in a style they call "campground gothic".

Personally I felt like you were

walking through a neighbourhood of pastel gingerbread houses.

It was quite lively though compared to other parts of the island. It had a Nashville honky-tonk feel to it with bars, shops and restaurants. I would check out the Offshore Ale Company, Madisons and Seasons Eatery and Pub.

To summarize Martha's Vineyard before moving onto Mac. I would describe it as a slightly backward, but picture perfect coastal island. A great "Get-away from it all" destination, especially in the winter months when the Atlantic unleashes its fury.

My advice would be to grab the place by the scruff of the neck and forget any snobbishness. The more effort you put in to seeing it all, the better experience you will have.

See everything, go everywhere and experience everything the Vineyard has to offer.

Mackinac Island is very similar to Martha's, but in contrast it is a destination given to you on a plate.

Off the northern tip of Michigan this island is much smaller than Martha's Vineyard covering only 3.8 square miles.

The island was home to Native Americans before European exploration began in the 17th century. It served as a strategic position amidst the commerce of the Great Lakes fur trade.

Later came the establishment of Fort Mackinac by the British during the American Revolutionary War.

VOTED FOR BY THE AUTHOR
BEST IN AMERICA
Fresh Unpolluted Air
Mackinac Island

Mackinac Island was one of the best surprises on my tour across America, as I had previously never heard of it.

On arrival the first surprise was the fact that the island does not allow motorized transportation, it was banned in 1898. So you have to travel everywhere either by foot, bike or in a horse-drawn taxi.

So after disembarking off the ferry on Main Street, filled with hotels, restaurants, souvenir and fudge shops. You will undoubtedly pop your bags on the horse drawn taxi and make your way to your hotel.

The novelty of no vehicles soon becomes apparent when you realize you can hear everyone's conversations as you ride up the street.

But you will also appreciate immediately the pristine clean-air and how quiet the place is.

It is so clean in fact that it has a slightly weird Wisteria Lane or Stepford Wives feel to it. I thought the whole Island was absolutely beautiful, as if built by the hand of Walt Disney himself.

I paid to stay at the expensive (but worth it) Grand Hotel. If you can stay or even just eat here I would recommend it. The Victorian architecture and views over the Island are outstanding.

Other Notable visitor attractions are Mackinac Fort and Marquette Park.

# Martha & Mac, MA & MI

Fort Mackinac, originally built in 1780, is a great spot for getting your bearings of the island. They have 14 original buildings and at the right time of the day you can hear the cannon, a bugle and rifle fire.

As if to frame the Fort, Marquette Park is the perfect spot for a picnic or just relaxing on the grass.

Also check out Benjamin's Blacksmith Shop and the historic houses dotted around the Island. Like Biddle House, McGulpin House, Mission House or Matthew Geary House.

Benjamin's Blacksmith Shop dates back to before 1885. It had been continuously operated by the Benjamin Family until 1968 when it was donated to the State Park Commission. Today you can get to see the art of being a blacksmith in the traditional way.

All of these attractions are fairly close to each other and give you a feel for what the island is all about and its history. So grab yourself a bike and map and go exploring.

I would also recommend picking-up the local newspaper, the Mackinac Island Town Crier which details events that week or head to the Visitor Centre.

Finally I would definitely recommend I pub crawl around Mackinac Island. I'm sure it could be the Most Condensed Pub Crawl in the World. As it only takes a short amount of time to walk or stagger from the 11 establishments.

My favourites where the Pink Pony, Yankee Rebel and Patrick Sinclair's Irish Pub. Don't be surprised though if you bump into your waiter or concierge from your hotel. This is a small island afterall!

Despite its small size there is plenty to do on Mackinac Island. I stayed there for a week and could easily have stayed a little longer.

I absolutely loved Mackinac Island, it was so pretty, pristine and traditional. It felt like you could have been stood in the 1800s.

Both Martha and Mac are very similar. Surrounded by the rugged coast with beautiful small villages, blue skies and pristinely clean.

I felt very lucky America had Voted for me to see them both. Both were idyllic and for some reason seem to be left off the tourist trail. If you get the chance to visit either, take it, you won't be disappointed.

# IF YOU HAVE MORE TIME ...

## Outdoors People

There are 20 Beaches dotted around Martha's Vineyard as well as around 67 trails and vistas. It is a great place for hiking, sea fishing and bike riding. For fishing head down to Oak Bluffs harbour and ask around to charter a boat for sport fishing off the coast of Martha's Vineyard.

On Mackinac, I would recommend taking a stroll to the top of Marquette Park and enjoy the views.

Alternatively tour one of its Lighthouses or visit Markinac State Park. Here you will find the pedestrian footpath for a direct route to Arch Rock.

## History, Culture & Gifts

Fancy splashing out, then then check out Nina McLemore's or Caryna Nina Boutique's Main Street and Summer Street in Edgartown. Nina is a NYC based designer and Caryna an established Haute Couture designer.
Also on Martha look out for the Farmers Markets, Artists Receptions and Antique Shows which happen on the weekends at Grange Hall, West Tisbury.

For that uniquely Mackinac gift go to Main Street to Martha's Sweet Shop or Sanders Candy. Or visit The Stewart House Museum which celebrates the Island's fur trade and its importance in Michigan's Great Lakes history.

## Photographers (People & Places)

At Oak Bluffs on Martha's Vineyard tucked behind circuit Avenue you will find the Methodist founded campground which was used as a retreat in 1835. Today it has more than 300 brightly decorated gingerbread cottages in a gothic style.

Built in 1780, Fort Mackinac attests to the Island's important place in American history. It also gives you panoramic views across the town, coast and park.

Needle Rock and the Grand Hotel also offer popular panoramic views of the island.

## Only in America.....

Martha's Vineyard is home to the flying horses carousel which is owned by the Martha's Vineyard preservation trust and listed in the National Register of Historic Places. It is the oldest continuously operated carousel in the country. This handcrafted carousel has been a feature on the vineyard since 1884.

A replica of the Statue of Liberty donated by the Boy Scouts of America sits in Haldimand Bay Mackinac Island. Or check out the Surrey Hills museum which showcases Mackinac's traditions with the horse and non motorized vehicles over the centuries.

# USA VOTED - TOP 6 'OTHER' LETTER "M" DESTINATIONS ...

**Mount Rushmore, South Dakota**
Distance to Rapid City Regional Airport is 32 miles or 50mins.

**Myrtle Beach, South Carolina**
Distance to Myrtle Beach International Airport is 4 miles or 10mins.

**Mammoth, California**
Distance to Klamath Falls Airport is 190 miles or approx. 1hr 55mins.

**Maui, Hawaii**
Distance to Kahului Airport is 13 miles or approx. 24mins.

**Madison (Sq. Garden) Ave & Manhattan, New York**
Distance to LaGuardia Airport is 11 miles or 21mins.

**Manhattan Beach, California**
Distance to Los Angeles International Airport 6 miles or 12mins

*N is for...... N* iagara Falls

**Niagara Falls, New York -** One of the World's most magical wonders straddling the Canadian and US borders. You can read and watch programmes about it, but until you have seen it up close. Nothing compares.

"N" is for Niagara Falls, New York (and Ontario). This had been the out and out winner throughout my trip across America. The only other place that came anywhere close in the Voting stakes was Nashville, Tennessee.

I won't go into the history or science of the falls too much, as there are hundreds of books and websites that can provide you with this kind of insight. Instead I will try to give you an understanding of how the falls feels and how being there fills up all of your senses.

Once you arrive, I would recommend visiting the Niagara USA official visitor centre which is located at 10 Rainbow Blvd, Niagara Falls, NY, 14303. They can provide you with all the important information before you get started.

The Niagara Falls are the most powerful waterfalls in North America, the next two most famous falls are probably Victoria Falls in Zambia and Iguazu Falls in Brazil. Niagara Falls situated on the Niagara River, drains Lake Erie into Lake Ontario which forms the international border between the Canadian province of Ontario and the U.S. state of New York.

Now there is some debate around "which side is better to see it on" having seen it on both, I hope to be able to give my perspective on this.

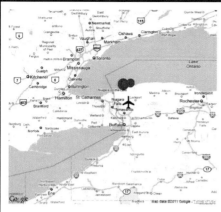

So first things first, getting there. It is true that the Ontario side is more geared up for the tourist and generally speaking if you get the chance to see the falls from one side or the other I would pick the Canadian.

However, this does not mean to say the New York side is bad, it is equally as good. So don't worry if you cannot get over to Canada. After all many parts of the world cannot because of visa restrictions.

Surprisingly places like the West Indies, Africa, South America, Russia, Asia and many parts of Europe. So check in case you need a tourist visa.

# Niagara Falls, New York

Considering approximately 13 million people visit each year. I am happy to announce that it is a very easy place to visit and there is normally plenty of parking. There is also a little shuttle trolley that will take you to the major attractions and look out points.

When you first arrive at Niagara Falls the first thing to listen out for is the noise. A noise that only gets louder as you get nearer the falls, its quite an alluring sound beckoning you in to "take a look".

Then when you get your first glimpse and match the thunderous sound with the image then "Wow". Look around you at the excited faces of the people you are with. I guarantee it is a sight to make your eyes light-up.

There are two major sections to the falls separated by Goat Island; the Horseshoe Falls on the Canadian side and the American Falls on the American side. The smaller Bridal Veil Falls are also located on the American side, separated from the main falls by Luna Island.

You will also undoubtedly see the Maid of the Mist, the boat so recognizable as belonging with Niagara Falls.

How long you stay standing there in awe will depend on how gob smacked you felt when you first saw them. Take your time, soak it up. Here are some of the key facts and figures as you do :

The water plummets down around 180ft at speeds up to 68 miles per hour. An average of 1,200,000 gallons (4,542,500 litres) of water a second.

Put in other terms that would be the equivalent of 2.2billion bottles of Coke or 1 million bath tubs a second.

With the force of the Falls it is estimated they are eroding at 1 foot per year. Niagara Falls also has its own man-made whirlpool.

Some of the things I saw were a surprise. One was how green the water is. Secondly, the amount of foam floating around on the top.

The green water is the result of decaying organics and minerals sometimes called Rock Flour.

The same algae plants and diatoms that give the water its fluorescent colour also contribute to the greyish foam you see floating on top as it mixes in the flowing rapids dissolving the calcium.

The Niagara Whirlpool was formed nearly 4,200 years ago when the Saint David's Buried Gorge ran perpendicular to the current path of the Fall's. The erosion resulted in a 90 degree turn in the river. Just upstream the narrow Niagara Gorge at the Whirlpool rapids sends water jetting into the Whirlpool basin.

When the Niagara River is at full flow the whirlpool will flow in a counter clockwise direction reaching depths of 125ft. When the river flow drops, diverted to the power plants, the flow of the whirlpool reverses (clockwise) creating this whirlpool effect. You can get a boat to ride them and get soaked if you like.

# Niagara Falls, New York

Whilst you are at the falls I would advise taking in as many activities as you can. The Maid of the Mist boat tour is a "must-do" and lasts about half an hour. If you have ever wondered what it would be like to go through a car wash, this is it. So take your sunglasses as eye protection, so you can see what's happening.

One of the advantages of the US side is that you can get up-close and personal to the falls in the Cave of the Winds where you get soaked just feet from the thundering waters.

Prospect Point is probably the other prime viewing area for the American Falls. With Observation Tower being the deck that extends out so you can see the Horseshoe Falls.

If you have the time and the budget I would book in advance and have dinner at any of the Top of the Falls restaurants. These will give you night time views of both sides of the falls.

My next recommendation would be the Daredevil Museum which is located on Rainbow Blvd Niagara Falls, NY. The one on the Ontario side is just a touristy sky-diving place, so skip it.

Here you can see daredevil memorabilia including Steve Trotter and Lori Martin's two-person barrel they used to survive the falls. Or the jet ski used in Robert Overakers attempt over the falls, which unsurprisingly killed him.

There have been 21 people who have tried to go over the falls as daredevils, 16 have survived and five have died.

The first person to go over the Horseshoe Falls and survive was Annie Edison Taylor in a barrel 1901. Let's hear it for the girls!

One man Kirk Jones, went over with nothing but the clothes on his back. A 7-year-old Roger Woodward accidentally went over the falls wearing a life preserver and survived in 1960. Sadly James Honeycutt, the driver of the boat he was in did not survive the drop.

On March 10, 2009 an unnamed man went over falls in a failed suicide attempt. Rescuers pulled him out completely naked, in shock and with a large gash on his head. He is the third person to ever survive the plunge without a craft.

Every year there are about a dozen suicides at the falls. Some change their minds at the last minute and require rescue. Others die; leaving authorities wondering if it was an intentional suicide or an attempt at becoming a famed Niagara Daredevil.

# N *is for......*  N iagara Falls

I had always thought it was an urban myth but it's true many people have tight-roped across Niagara Falls.

The most famous is Jean Francois Gravelot, better know as The Great Blondin. He was born in 1824 in Northern France.

He became obsessed with crossing the Niagara River on a tightrope.

He was finally successful on June 30th 1859.

But not satisfied with that, during the summer of 1859, Blondin completed it 8 more times. His most bizarre crossing occurred in the August when unbelievably he carried his manager Harry Colcord on his back. Imagine that conversation "Monsieur Harry, I have an idea..."

During the summer of 1860, Blondin returned to Niagara for a second successful year of tight rope walking for hundreds of thousands of sightseers. One of his acts included pushing a wheelbarrow along as he crossed. Blondin died in 1897 at the age of 73. These French, "they do like to show off!"

Signorina Maria Spelterini was the first woman to ever cross the Niagara River gorge on a tight rope. She was a 23 year old buxom, 150 pound beautiful woman of Italian descent. She crossed wearing peach baskets strapped to her feet.

Not satisfied with that on July 19th 1876, she decided to cross blind folded.

Then on July 22nd 1876, Spelterini crossed with her ankles and wrists manacled. These Italian's, "they're crazy!"

You may have sensed I got fascinated by these so called "Daredevils" and seeing the falls in all its glory made their exploits so much more impressive.

So I would encourage you to go to the Daredevil Museum.

If you come across any books about them, buy one because they are an amusing read and hard to get hold of anywhere else.

I am not sure what it is that brings people to Niagara Falls. It could be a romantic notion, or perhaps to learn more about the science and history of the place.

To hear the stories of the heroic daredevils. Or simply to hear the constant roar of the falls and get soaked underneath them. Or maybe it is to reminisce in the traditions like the Maid of the Mist.

Whatever your reason for coming, there is one thing for sure. Niagara Falls will light up your senses as you stand in awe and wonderment at its immense power.

# IF YOU HAVE MORE TIME ...

## Outdoors People

There are over 11 State or Recreational Parks in the area. The Davor Woods State Park offers a playground, hiking trail, wildflower area picnic tables and grills as well as the footpath that connects to Whirlpool State Park and the Robert Moses's trail.

Hyde Park offers many recreational activities like swimming, volleyball, baseball, indoor ice skating, tennis, a golf course as well as picnicking and hiking trails. From here you are close to Whirlpool State Park where you can walk, run or bike the multi-use trail.

For spectacular vista views, hike along the Niagara Gorge Rim Trail. Or for more difficult and challenging hikes there are stairs that descend to a trail along the river's raging edge.

## History, Culture & Gifts

Visit Niagara launch Discovery Centre. Through interactive displays and a multiscreen presentation you'll see how rivers and lakes feed into Niagara Falls.

NACRO is New York State's largest multi-arts Centre. This facility has galleries, gift shops and a cafe opened to the public. The Art Parks is the perfect venue to see a concert. Overlooking the Niagara River Gorge and features a 2,400 seat main stage theatre and lawn seating, minutes from the Falls.

Looking for a unique gift then welcome aboard Liberty Excursions–the Black Pearl. Experience sailing in a 1948 classic wooden tall ship on the Lower Niagara or Lake Ontario.

## Photographers (People & Places)

I would get myself to Devils or Whirl Pool State Park it offers some spectacular views of the vistas along the Niagara Gorge Rim Trail.

Or for a completely different photography subject away from water. I would head to the Fatima Shrine which is 15 acres of gardens highlighted by a glass dome basilica and a 13 foot statue of our Lady of Fatima. Here you will find natural ponds as well as beautiful gardens.

I would also check out old Fort Niagara this early 18th century fortress was active during the French and Indian War, the American Revolution and the War of 1812. Provides exciting living history programmes, exhibits and spectacular scenery.

## Only in America.....

Daredevil Museum located on 303 Rainbow Blvd. If you were thinking of considering becoming a Daredevil over Niagara Falls. Or find yourself accidentally falling in, be mindful that it will set you back at least $10,000 in fines plus the costs for your rescue. Imagine if it was a suicide attempt and you lost your bottle. How "down in the dumps" would you be after having to pay that!

Don't fancy the drop yourself then head to Niagara Adventure Theatre –45ft IMAX. You can plunge over the falls with histories daredevils without getting wet. Check out www.niagaramovie.com

Ransomville Speedway - is an open wheel stock car track. Racing occurs Friday evenings, May through September.

# USA VOTED - TOP 6 'OTHER' LETTER "N" DESTINATIONS ...

### Napa Valley, California
Distance to Oakland International Airport is 53 miles or approx. 1hr 4mins.

### New Orleans, Louisiana
Distance to Louis Armstrong International Airport is 13 miles or 19mins.

### Nashville, Tennessee
Distance to Nashville International Airport is 8 miles or 15miles.

### Nantucket, Massachusetts
Distance to Logan International Airport is 103 miles or approx. 2hrs.

### Natchitoches, Louisiana
Distance to George Bush Intercontinental Airport is 215 miles or approx. 4hrs 7mins.

### Naples, Florida
Distance to Naples Municipal Airport is 4 miles or 10mins.

# *O* is for...... *O*gunquit

**Ogunquit, Maine -** Is a quintessentially picture postcard American coastal resort on the blustery Atlantic coast. With Maine being fondly known as a "mecca" for lighthouses enthusiasts.

Maine has over 3,500 miles of indescribably beautiful coastline, enticing you with summer cottages, craggy cliffs and scenic ocean vistas. With a strong maritime connection it is fondly known as a Mecca for lighthouse enthusiasts with over 60 along the coast line.

No surprises it is famed for its fresh seafood, due to all the cool, clear waters which provide the perfect environment. Approximately 40 million pounds (nearly 90 per cent) of the nation's lobster supply is caught off the coast of Maine. But here is a surprising fact, Maine also produces 99% of all the blueberries in the United States.

I had a beautiful journey away from Niagara heading south to the alpine village of Lake Placid in New York State. Then through two states to Champlain Lake at Burlington, Vermont onto Boston then Salem, Massachusetts. Before heading north up along the Maine coast to Ogunquit.

Ogunquit is a quintessentially picture postcard American seaside resort, with images so perfect you can imagine they would appear on tins of biscuits or candy. I came across this type of resort on numerous occasions across America. If you like Ogunquit then you will like places like Chatham in New England, St. Pete's Beach in Florida, The Hampton's, New York or Hilton Head, South Carolina to name but a few.

USA - Northeast Region

Ogunquit with its rugged coast-line, white picket fenced town and coastal walkways is a perfect vacation spot in the summer. Not too hot at the height of summer but chilly through fall and freezing in winter.

Personally I would recommend visiting in the late Spring or early Fall. It will be quite blustery, ideal to see the waves crashing against the coastal inlets. Perfect to remind you why you like soup and hearty stews!

Ogunquit meant Coastal Lagoon to native Abenaki Indians which first settled within the town of Wells in 1641.

# Ogunquit, Maine

Nowadays the town of Ogunquit, is referred to as the "Beautiful Place by the Sea" nestled into the southern Maine coastline. A relatively new town it was incorporated in 1980, having separated from Wells. It has a small year round population of just under 5,000 people.

Nearby and a "must see" is the bewitching Perkins Cove. Originally created as a safe anchorage from Atlantic storms it is still a working fishing harbour today.

Here you can take a walk along a scenic footpath of the rocky coastline that joins the harbour to the village. Whilst enjoying a bowl of hot clam chowder you can take in the many gift shops, restaurants and enjoy the stunning views.

Ogunquit over the years has been famous for shipbuilding, timber, fishing and the arts. But nowadays tourism has taken over with large hotels and guest houses accommodating the thousands of visitors who come each summer.

I suggest getting a B&B or hotel alittle out of town nearer to Wells and parking-up. Then taking the very handy trolley that runs between Wells, Perkins Cove and Ogunquit. Which stops at all the major attractions with a very helpful and knowledgeable driver.

You could easily spend a week here with the whole family, young to old. I saw lots of families when I visited enjoying a range of activities, as well as a handful of marriages.

It also seemed very popular with Canadian's who head south to get away from their torrid winters. Google search: Ogunquit Guidebook for more information.

I really enjoyed visiting the State of Maine it has a reserved calm about it, something you don't get in many other states.

The seafood as well was the best I tasted, only matched in Alaska and Martha's Vineyard. So you should come to Maine just to have some Chowder or Lobster!

The fact that Ogunquit was Voted my highest letter "O" lays testament to its popularity. It goes to underline how beautiful it is.

It is the type of place that once you have visited "Stays with You" and chances are you will be back ...

# IF YOU HAVE MORE TIME ...

## Outdoors People

Maine contains over 500 thousand acres of State and National parks, including the 92-mile Allagash Wilderness Waterway in northern Maine. Acadia National Park is one of America's most visited National Parks. Just for the record, from my experience I found every National Park and National Park Service Unit were definitely worth a visit. The Great Smoky Mountains being the most popular.

Maine Boasts 6,000 lakes, 5,100 rivers and streams. It has more than 25 ski areas, including nationally-known Sugarloaf, USA. So you are never far from outdoor activities and worth further research depending on your base location.

There are around 10 golf clubs within driving distance of Ogunquit, I would go to Cape Neddick Country Club. Check out : www.hydigolfschool.com

## History, Culture & Gifts

Life at Sea is entwined into the history of Maine. The Sailor's Memorial Museum in Isleboro or The Penobscot Marine Museum in Searsport has numerous historic buildings and marine memorabilia.

Also Ogunquit Museum of American Art and the Heritage Museum are worth an afternoon visit if the weather turns sour.

Freeport, Maine has managed to retain its village feel, despite the influx of major retailers. It is the home to the outdoor & hunting retailer L.L. Bean Company. Located on Main Street the locks on the doors were removed in 1951, opening 24 hours a day year-round. Today, more than 3 million shoppers visitors each year.

## Photographers (People & Places)

Numerous lighthouses dot the Maine coast. Although it can be blustery, these offer some of the best photography opportunities. I would check out Fort Point Lighthouse in Stockton Springs and Grindle Point Lighthouse on Isleboro.

If you are into lighthouses, then this whole coastline from Massachusetts up is considered lighthouse 'mecca'. There are well over 40 in Maine for you to research further.

If you go sailing I would recommend docking into the fishing port Boothbay Harbor which offers great scenery and a 128-acre Botanical Gardens for a completely different subject.

## Only in America ...

Located in Thorndike Village, the Bryant Stove Works and Museum displays an eclectic collection of antique roadsters and touring cars. In addition, the museum features antique layer pianos, pipe organs and music boxes, calliopes, nickelodeons (jukebox) and hurdy-gurdys (a musical instrument).

The Maine coastline boasts so many deep harbours it is thought all the Navies in the world could anchor in them.

Maine also has more Moose per mile than any other state. The Moose is the State animal.

# USA VOTED - TOP 6 'OTHER' LETTER "O" DESTINATIONS ...

**Orlando, Florida**
Distance to Orlando International Airport is 12 miles or 21mins.

**Ouray, Colorado**
Distance to Telluride Regional Airport is 47 miles or approx. 1hr 5mins.

**Orange County, California**
Distance to Los Angeles International Airport is 36 miles or 42miles.

**Ocean City, Maryland**
Distance to Baltimore/Washington Airport is 134 miles or 2hrs.

**Old Orchard, Maine**
Distance to Portland International airport is 16 miles or approx. 21mins

**Outer Banks, North Carolina**
Distance to First Flight Airport is 35 miles or approx. 50mins.

# *P* *is for......* *P*agosa Springs

**Pagosa Springs, Colorado-** For a weekend away to 'de-stress' with other adults, this is the perfect location. Visit when the weather is cool so you can fully appreciate the snowy landscape and bubbling hot spa pools.

Letter "P" is for Pagosa Springs, Colorado. Of all the states I went across I used to really enjoy going through Colorado. It was stunning anytime of the year with some of the best outdoors scenery in the whole of the US. Colorado - Welcome to the Great Outdoors.

The State is framed around the 14,000 foot San Juan National Forest and Rocky Mountains commonly known as the Fourteeners by locals. As if to reaffirm its beauty Colorado was the inspiration for Katherine Lee Bates poem America the Beautiful after a trip to the summit of Pikes Peak. For the non-American readers this is the "other" famed National Anthem, normally sang first at the Super Bowl.

Whether traveling the Million Dollar Highway to the wild-west Lake City, the mountain ranges at Elk Mountain or idling through the pastures and woodlands of Aspen. Colorado offers an outdoor lifestyle for skiing (over 36 ski-resorts), fishermen, grand rapid enthusiasts and surprisingly it seems lots and lots of cyclists.

The location of Pagosa Springs is in the south western part of Colorado. This area is packed full of history about mountain men, frontier lands and trying to strike it rich on silver or gold. In recognition of this, many of Colorado's towns are in the States Register of Historic Places and therefore have some fascinating museums.

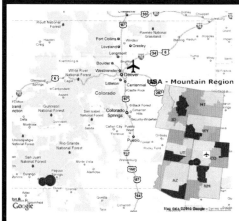

USA - Mountain Region

Its history started with the horse and wagon then the railroad which played an important part in the development of Colorado.

As a testament to this, there is an event that occurs annually in the spring. Which pitches "Man Against Machine" called The Iron Horse Bicycle Classic. It is a three and a half hour race from Durango to Silverton originally started in 1972.

Covering 49.7 miles over two gruelling mountain passes it pitches cyclists against an old steam train along the Animas River. I won't spoil it by telling you who usually wins!

# Pagosa Springs, Colorado

I loved driving around Colorado, the scenery is fantastic and there is plenty to see and do. Here are some of my recommendations within driving distance of Pagosa:

Worth a visit is Messa Verde an 82 square mile National Park preserving the works of prehistoric man and 4,000 Ancestral Puebloans sites built into the cliffs.

I would also check out Telluride which has become the perfect place to "chill out" and enjoy the many festivals that occur throughout the year. But it is transformed in the winter to a ski-mecca. With well over 1,000 acres of ski-able terrain and 65 trails it is known throughout the world as a prestigious ski resort.

Ski and snowboard enthusiasts should also check out the aptly named Purgatory which is less well known (so cheaper) but just as much fun.

Strangely Purgatory Colorado, and Hell in Montana were Voted for quite a lot by many Americans. I thought I had been "quite good company" so I thought it strange how many of them wanted to send me to places of damnation!

As Colorado's second biggest City after the capital Denver, I would visit Colorado Springs. It is the proud home of the US Olympic Committee and has the city's US Olympic Training Centre which you can visit. Being centrally located it offers a training location for athletes from around the country.

But the highlight, or low-light depending on how you look at it, was a visit to the city of Fruita. Fruita, Colorado holds a festival in honour of one of its infamous residents "Mike the Headless Chicken".

"Mike" the original headless chicken celebrates his Birthday on the 5th of May at the Headless Chicken Festival. The festival is a two day poultry party featuring a highly amusing chicken-clucking competition as well as a wing eating contest.

You have to check out the "Run Like A Chicken With Your Head Cut Off" 5K run and Lawnmower Hockey using a rubber chicken instead of a puck. Yes this really is true, I am not making it up!

Wannabe new fans of "Mike the Headless Chicken" can become his friend on Facebook were Mike has over 4,000 fans. Who said American's don't have a sense of humour!

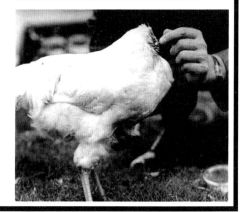

The best way to describe Pagosa Springs is for you to shut your eyes and imagine it for a minute. You are sat in 1 of 12 naturally formed hot bubbling pool's with the healing properties of sulphate, calcium, fluoride, zinc and iron.

All ranging in temperature from warm to extremely hot. Whilst overlooking the cold Rio Grande river rushing by as you take in large gulps of the crisp, clean, fresh Colorado air. Arr...and relax...

For anyone who enjoys spa treatments, this must be considered "Spa Heaven".

# Pagosa Springs, Colorado

The even funnier thing is that all the locals look like they belong in the film Cocoon or all have Orange County Plastic surgeons in the family. There is definitely something in the water in Pagosa Springs!

The Native American tribes knew this, they had numerous battles to try to control Pagosah which means "boiling waters". In 1866 there was one final battle between the Navajo and Utes to decide who would take ultimate control. The Ute's came out as victors. Today it is owned by The Springs Resort & Spa.

I visited a handful of these spa locations across the US like Hot Springs, Virginia, Palm Springs, California and Thermopolis, Wyoming. But they were not a patch on the Springs Resort.

As for the town itself it offers many quaint shops and wonderful places to eat and drink. On Pagosa's Main Street I ate in some great restaurants. I would recommend Victoria's Cafe which was a delightful English tea shop.

Plus I had a great welcome and BBQ at Boss Hog's which offers a range of chicken, pork and steak combinations. I also had The Best Vegetarian (Spinach) Lasagna in America at Bacci's Italian restaurant a small drive away.

One memorable night in particular, I spent the evening at the Beaver's Lounge. Where I was delighted to be spontaneously entertained by local musicians (Johnny & Val) who just popped in the bar. Val came in with a guitar made from a cigar box he had created that afternoon.

Sat with them my knowledge of blues, folk and bluegrass tripled by the time I had left. These guys also inspired me to buy a guitar and learn to play it on my journey across the States. I don't think I'll ever be as good as them though.

I was soon to discover the whole area around Pagosa is alive with many artists and musicians. Joni Mitchell (I was told) has made a home in the area and performs at the numerous festivals that take place throughout the year. Including the Pagosa Folk and Bluegrass Festival and the South Fork Festival to name just two.

So that was Colorado and Pagosa Springs. If you are looking for the Fountain of Youth or just a weekend away to 'de-stress' with other adults there is no-where better.

4th Annual
Pagosa Folk 'N Bluegrass
June 3-5, 2011
Reservoir Hill Park
Pagosa Springs, CO

# IF YOU HAVE MORE TIME ...

## Outdoors People

Check out the 2,000 foot Black Canyon and the Gunnison National Monument encompassing some 13,000 (+) acres. No other canyon in North America has the depth, narrowness and sheerness of the Black Canyon. Which many climbers attempt each year.

Pikes Peak and the Devils Playground trail offer challenging hikes to elevations of over 7,000ft with spectacular alpine views. Named after this Army Lieutenant (who's name I love) Zebulon Montgomery Pike. There are also numerous trails around the Rocky Mountain National Park which are worth checking out. With spectacular scenery, beautiful wildflowers, cascading waterfalls and beautiful alpine lakes. My recommendations: Glacier Gorge, Indian Peaks Wilderness, Bergen Peak and Maroon Bells Snowmass.

## History, Culture & Gifts

To the south of Cortez is the 825,000 acre Ute Tribe Native American reservation. It is home to their ancestral Puebloan sites which can be visited with a guide.

Lake City has more than 75 buildings that date back to the 1800's making it look like it belongs in a western. Or head south of Lake City to Colorado's second largest natural lake the San Cristobal which is stunningly beautiful.

Mesa Verde and Black Mesa are definitely worth further research and a visit to trace its pre-historic antiquity.

## Photographers (People & Places)

The Garden of the Gods is a series of rock formations that date back 17 million years. The vertical fins of the different rocks offer a multicolored backdrop to a hike or ride.

Or check out the Paint Mines at Calhan. The clay formations create a natural sculpture garden with a rainbow of colors created by the minerals being eroded by wind and water in the canyon.

Also fun to photograph is the United States Air Force Academy located in Colorado Springs. I thought the building was architecturally stunning and worth photographing.

## Only in America.....

In Fruita, the town folk celebrate 'Mike the Headless Chicken Day'. A farmer named L.A. Olsen cut off Mike's head on September 10, 1945 in anticipation of a chicken dinner - but Mike survived and lived for another 4 years without a head. Poor Mike!

Loveland, Colorado is perhaps best known nationwide as the home of the Valentine Re-Mailing Program. Every year, hundreds of thousands of Valentines are sent to Loveland. They get repackaged inside larger envelopes by volunteers who hand-stamp them with a Loveland stamp and Valentine's verse then send them on to their intended recipients.

# USA VOTED - TOP 6 'OTHER' LETTER "P" DESTINATIONS ...

### Palm Springs, Florida
Distance to Palm Springs International Airport is 3 miles or 7mins.

### Panama City, Florida
Distance to Northwest Florida Beaches International Airport is 22 miles or 37 minutes.

### Park City, Utah
Distance to Salt Lake City International Airport is 47 miles or 56mins.

### Page, Arizona
Distance to Flagstaff Pulliam Airport is 140 miles or approx. 2hrs 37mins.

### Paradise, Michigan
Distance to Sawyer International Airport is 138 miles or 2hrs 45mins.

### Put-In-Bay, Ohio
Distance to Put-In-Bay Airport is 2 miles or 10mins.

# *Q* is for......    # *Q*uincy

**Quincy, Florida -** Quincy was established in the year 1823 and has an interesting history around tobacco growing and Coca-Cola. With an unusually high percentage of African Americans choosing to call it Home.

"Q" is for Quincy, Florida. It turns out there are more than 8 Quincy's dotted across the US in the States of Washington, Pennsylvania, Massachusetts, Kentucky, Kansas, Illinois, Florida and California. It got the second highest Votes after Queens, NY but I couldn't include Queens in the book as it is a major city and has two international airports. Sorry Queens, rules are rules!

If you ever get the chance to visit Queens I think it will surprise you, I expected it to be quite urban and earthy. But to my complete surprise the main downtown area is like Tokyo or Hong Kong. With neon signs lining the streets with Chinese writing and lots of small business owners and restaurants all crammed together. If you are familiar with Korea Town in Los Angeles, you will know what I mean.

I know that the rest of the world thinks that people from the USA have somewhat questionable geography knowledge and don't have passports. Officially America offers no vacation time only public holidays so I can see why they wouldn't have passports. As for the geography, I can confirm from my experience it can be true.

The number of American's who when I asked them for a letter "Q" in the United States said "Quebec" was very amusing. At first I just let it slide, but after a while I felt I should correct them and remind them that it is in fact in Canada ......Bless!

Having been to many Quincy's I came across a strange phenomenon. That Quincy, Washington was very similar to Quincy, Pennsylvania. Just like Quincy, Kentucky is similar to Quincy in Kansas. Quincy in California is very similar to Quincy in Florida and Quincy, Massachusetts is was a very similar to Quincy Illinois.

It was as if there had been some secret collusion going on. It was quite spooky to go from Quincy to Quincy and find such similarity despite them being dotted all across the USA.

# Quincy, Florida

All the people who voted for Quincy I think did so because of the old 1970s pathologist TV show. Or they knew there was a Quincy somewhere in America, but they were not sure which state.

With this in mind and to try to be true to their Votes I visited as many Quincy's as I could and then decided which one would be best to put in the book. So may I introduce to you Quincy, Florida.

It is a small town in the north of the state close to the state line with Georgia. The nearest city is Tallahassee and it has a population of just under 7,000 people.

The area known as Quincy holds a seat in Gadsden county, established in the year 1823. The county was named in honour of James Gadsden of South Carolina, who served as Florida's aide-de-camp (assistant) in the year 1818.

The City of Quincy itself was named in honour of John Quincy Adams and was established in 1828 by Governor P.DuVal who introduced tobacco to the territory of Florida.

Tobacco has long been a dominant factor in the social and economic development of the county. In 1829, an important man in the history of Quincy named John Smith migrated to Gadsden County.

As there was already a resident named John Smith in the community, he became known as John 'Virginia' Smith. This was because be brought Virginia and Cuban tobacco seeds to Quincy.

Once blended they became a cigar called the Florida Wrapper. Growing tobacco continued to be profitable until the beginning of the Civil War in 1861.

Since then it has peaked and troughed under governmental, social, technology and price pressures. The last crop of shade-grown Cigar Wrapper tobacco was grown in 1977.

Quincy then turned to other agriculture like tomatoes, mushrooms and egg farms.

The main square in Quincy is only a few blocks circling around the County Courthouse. You can walk around it quite comfortably and it is a nice stroll. It reminded me somewhat of the Town Hall square in the film Back to the Future.

Interestingly, the African American population is well above the 12.9% US average at around 64% and it is apparent when walking around town.

I arrived on a Sunday so everyone was decked-out in their Sunday Best having just come from church.

There is one thing I have found about African Americans is that they always seem to dress immaculately. The matching of every tie, shoe, hat to handbag seems somehow engrained within their DNA.

So I followed the crowds into Divine Grace just next to the beautiful Courthouse building. It was like walking into a church hall wedding with long tables, paper tables cloths and a large buffet queue at one end.

## Quincy, Florida

One thing I had learnt about my trips through Mississippi and Louisiana is that people from the South or near a Bayou certainly know how to cook.

Although I was the only white face in the crowd of over a hundred I was offered a nice welcome and was looking forward to joining the queue to see what delights awaited me. It didn't disappoint.

Firstly, to drink there was a choice of sweet iced tea and freshly squeezed lemonade served in 10 gallon dispensing containers.

But it was the food that was the star attraction. Fried chicken, squash, corn, green beans, rice & peas, mashed potato, biscuits, goat stew and various types of gravy.

Served with a side of The Best Corn Bread I have ever tasted in my life. Light and fluffy, it was somewhere in-between a potato cake and a pancake.

The smell alone had been worth the 10 minute line. So I sat and ate my food, with the odd stare from locals thinking "who is this strange white English girl in our midst?" Anyway after a huge tip and a final glug of lemonade, so sweet it made your teeth stand on end. I was back into the humid summer heat of Florida.

VOTED FOR BY THE AUTHOR
**BEST IN AMERICA**
Fried Chicken & Cornbread
Divine Grace, N Madison Street
Quincy, Florida

I had a walk-around and fell across a small shop front adorned with numerous Martin Luther King pictures and sculptors. Being a Sunday it was closed, but I later found out this had been a museum to mark Martin Luther King Jnr. Day.

I also came across some Coca-Cola murals on a wall in the town square. The type that if they where in London, someone would have stolen the whole wall to cash-in on the potential value of Americana history. Ala Banksy. I was therefore intrigued to find out the Coca- Cola history. Quincy was once rumoured to be home to many millionaires due to the Coca-Cola boom. Pat Munroe and W.C. Bradley were among the stockholders of 3 banks that released 500,000 shares of the new Coca-Cola stock. They urged widows and farmers to invest for $40 each. Eventually that stock split making 67 investors rich. To give you an idea of the stock's value, 1 share of Coca-Cola stock bought in 1919 for $100 would supposedly today be worth $12.5 million..

So that was my whistle-stop tour of Quincy, Florida. Don't think I'll be rushing back, but amazing food and nice people.

# IF YOU HAVE MORE TIME ...

## Outdoors People

There are 4 State parks close-by to Quincy, the Alfred B Maclay State Gardens, Edward Ball Wakulla, Springs State Park and the Three Rivers State Park. I visited The Alfred B Maclay State Gardens, they were a set of beautifully designed gardens and certainly worth a visit if you enjoy gardening.

Golf courses include the Havana Golf & Country Club, The Jake Gaither Golf Course and Golf Club of Quincy. You can get further information from here: Americantowns/gadsden-county

## History, Culture & Gifts

There are lots of museums and places to visit in the local region, here are my recommendations:

- The Tallahassee Museum of History and Natural Science—features lots of animals, its more like a zoo than a museum.

- Museum of Florida - shows the history of the State of Florida, featuring art works and fossil exhibitions.

- Knott House Museum - this is a great example of an early pioneer and Victorian mansion, originally owned by Luella and William Knott a poet and politician.

## Photographers (People & Places)

The Leaf Theatre (named after the city's tobacco fame) still holds performances throughout the year. Check out the local paper: The Gadsden County Times. It is also rumoured to be haunted and the Leaf Theatre sponsors a walk through in which they feature ghost stories.

There are some fantastic Queen-Anne Victorian pioneer homes that have been converted into bed and breakfasts on the outskirts of Quincy. Not only are they great to stay at, but the architecture of these brightly coloured homes with classic period porches is stunning. Check out: Allison House Inn and McFarlin House.

## Only in America.....

Quincy's courthouse is allegedly haunted as it was infamous for being the site of many hangings of criminals in the past.

Plant City, Florida is the Winter Strawberry Capital of the World. It holds the Guinness Book of Records for the world's largest strawberry shortcake. The 827 square-foot, 6,000 pound cake was made on Feb. 19, 1999 in McCall Park.

Once a year, thousands of Floridians stand at the state line and toss dead fish into Alabama. It's the annual Mullet Toss hosted by Flora-Bama Beach Bar in Pensacola. In other words it's just "a silly excuse for another huge Florida beach party."

# USA VOTED - TOP 6 'OTHER' LETTER "Q" DESTINATIONS ...

**Queens, New York**
Distance to JFK Airport is 9 miles or approx. 16mins.

**Quakertown, Pennsylvania**
Distance to Lehigh Valley International Airport is 28 miles or 34mins.

**Quartzsite, Arizona**
Distance to Phoenix Sky Harbor International Airport is 136 miles or 2hrs 11mins.

**Quechee State Park, Vermont**
Distance to Lebanon Municipal Airport is 9 miles or 16mins.

**Quantico, Vermont**
Distance to Stafford Regional Airport is 18 miles or approx. 35mins.

**Quitman, Texas**
Distance to Wood County Airport is 6 miles or 8mins.

# $R$ *is for......* $R$ehoboth

**Rehoboth Beach, Delaware -** This quaint Victorian seaside resort is a perfect weekend get-away. Good bars, restaurants and clean beaches all within walking distance of your accommodation.

"R" is for Rehoboth Beach, Delaware which just beat Richmond, Virginia to the top spot in Votes. It reminded me of many of the coastal resorts I have visited across the US. Places like Huntington Beach, California, Panama City, Florida, Myrtle Beach, South Carolina or Orange Beach, Alabama. All are seaside resorts and geared-up for the vacationing traveller.

The city was founded in 1873 as the Rehoboth Beach Camp Meeting Association by the Rev. Robert W. Todd of the St. Paul's Methodist Episcopal Church of Wilmington, Delaware. Originally it was used for Methodist Camp meetings, today it caters for families, fraternity outings, bikers and surf dudes.

Affectionally known as "The Nation's Summer Capital" due to the fact that it is a frequent summer vacation destination for Washington, D.C. residents as well as visitors from Maryland, Virginia and Pennsylvania.

What is nice about Rehoboth is that unlike many of these resorts that have become over commercialized and decided to cater for the Spring Break fraternity crowds, hence losing their family seaside charm. Rehoboth has managed to get the balance just right, where tradition meets tacky and the greasy boardwalk competes with fine dining. Meaning you get a nice mix of people who come to enjoy the sun and have fun.

Like Arkansas I got the impression that most American's know very little about the State of Delaware. So when it came to Rehoboth most didn't have a predisposed opinion about it either way. As people know very little about it, they are pleasantly surprised when they visit.

When you first arrive most people check in and make their way down towards the beach. Passing the quaint Victorian seaside holiday homes on the way.

The beach is immaculate, right next to the boardwalk, which still maintains its Victorian landmarks like Dollies (candy store), the Plaza Hotel and original Bandstand.

# Rehoboth, Delaware

Speaking of The Boardwalk Plaza Hotel, if you are looking for a romantic get-away I would certainly recommend a stay at the Plaza. Or get dressed-up and at least Have Tea, it is very nice. Reminded me just a tad of The Ritz, London where I once had afternoon tea with my Mum many moons ago.

Rehoboth Beach has that Mediterranean strolling feeling to it. One should not be bar hopping, guzzling down beer, doughnuts and pizza. But instead should be leisurely reading a book, enjoying the weather, before preparing oneself for dinner in a nice restaurant.

There are many restaurants to choose from, the beauty of Rehoboth Beach is that once you have parked the car and checked in you can pretty much walk around everywhere you need to go. After all, according to the 2010 census, the population is only about 1,327.

So that evening I chose to eat at the Blue Moon Restaurant which I had booked the night before on Justin Smith's (a Rehoboth native) recommendation. "Good choice, thanks Justin".

They have their own House-Made Charcuterie made up of Foie Gras, Duck Rillette, Sausage (etc) which would not look out of place in a rustic country restaurant in France. As well as Sweetbreads and Slow Roasted Suckling Pig.

I decided to stick with American, having spent many a summer in France and Spain.

I had the Rockfish and Chestnut-Apple soup to start, made with parsnips, vanilla salt and maple reduction. Then the Amish Chicken which came with croquettes, whipped potatoes, kale and a maple glaze.

Having spent some time with the Amish communities in Pennsylvania and Illinois I wanted to experience the slightly ironic 'fine dining' version of it. It was all very delicious, top marks to the guys at Blue Moon. Shame about the 1980s through-back name!

So that was Rehoboth, after a week of chilling out, great food and weather it was time to say "cheerio" having seen and done most things.

To sum up Rehoboth Beach it is the perfect American beach vacation destination, without a tacky souvenir shop or lager lout in sight.

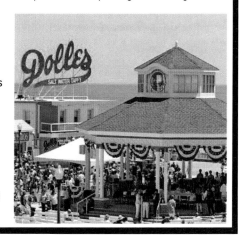

## Outdoors People

Rehoboth Beach Boarding School offer surf lessons throughout the summer. www.boardingschoolrb.com. Or how about getting yourself one of those ridiculous stand-up Paddle Boards you see people using in the sea. Go to Liquid in Rehoboth or go on-line at: www.liquidboard.com.
Captain K's (no relation) Fishing does trips everyday but Thursday leaving at 8 a.m. (4 hrs) from the Rusty Rudder, Dewey Beach. Surf fishing is also popular in Rehoboth the most popular spots are Tower Road, Indian River Inlet, Cape Henlopen Point and the Navy Jetty area within Cape Henlopen State Park.
Crabbing lessons occur Saturdays at 1 p.m at the fishing pier at Cape Henlopen State Park in Lewes. Get your equipment at Hoss Bait & Tackle.

## History, Culture & Gifts

Humans probably inhabited the area of Rehoboth Beach as long ago as 10,000 BC. At that time, sea levels were lower and the Atlantic Coast lay about 30 miles farther east than today. By the time the first Europeans arrived in the area in the 17th century, the English (hooray!) and Dutch settlers radiated outward from Delaware forcing the Native Tribes to migrate North (boo!).

Believe it or not, Delaware provides tax-free shopping in many parts of the State. Some of the shops in Rehoboth offer this, so Downtown Rehoboth Beach has over 200 boutique shops. There is so much shopping in fact, there is too much to mention in one paragraph. I'll be the one stood outside, looking bored. Rosie!

## Photographers (People & Places)

The town has several festivals including the Sea Witch Halloween and Fiddlers Festival. Similar to a Love Parade or Carnival it normally takes place in October and features amongst other things competitions for Banjo, Fiddle and Bluegrass artists. Not forgetting the Best Costumed Pet Contest for Dogs, Cats, and Other Pets?? (goodness knows what that means? Lions?)

There is also the Rehoboth Beach Independent Film Festival in the Fall. A five-day Festival showcasing hundreds of the best American and international films (features, documentaries, and shorts) at one, multi-screen location. Or check out the Rehoboth Beach Autumn Jazz Festival every year.

## Only in America.....

Rehoboth Beach is known as one of the mid-Atlantic coast's popular gay and lesbian getaways. This is because of the large number of gay-owned and operated businesses in the area. Not to mention the aptly named Poodle Beach near Queen Street. No, I am not making this up! The tourist book says "It is this stretch of the beach that gay people frequent". So don't forget to bring your rainbow beach umbrella! I thought this was quite amusing, only in America would segregation be considered normal! Whatever next a beach where "men who like talking football, can frequent!"

Delaware is the only state without any National Park System units such as national parks, seashores, historic sites or battlefields. memorials, and monuments.

# USA VOTED - TOP 6 'OTHER' LETTER "R" DESTINATIONS ...

**Richmond, Virginia**
Distance to Richmond International Airport is 9 miles or approx. 17mins.

**Redondo Beach, California**
Distance to Los Angeles International Airport is 8 Miles or 13mins.

**Roanoke Island, North Carolina**
Distance to Franklin Municipal Airport is 136 miles or 1hr 11mins.

**Rocky Point, Hawaii**
Distance to Dillingham Airport is 9 miles or 16mins.

**Reno, Nevada**
Distance to Reno International Airport is 5 miles or approx. 10mins.

**Raleigh, North Carolina**
Distance to Raleigh International Airport is 17 miles or 27mins.

# $S$ _is for......_ $S$edona

**Sedona, Arizona -** Release the skeptic in you and open your mind to Sedona's spiritual and healing properties. Venture into a Vortex to connect with nature in this truly unique destination.

"S" is for Sedona, Arizona. The letter "S" produced two early front-runners in the Voting stakes on my A to Zee journey. Savannah, Georgia and Sedona, Arizona, continued to be the highest voted "S" destinations throughout my journey. In the end Savannah won, with Sedona coming a close second. But under The Rules Savannah has a population well over 100 thousand and an international airport so would be consider a major city and therefore could not appear in the book. Making Sedona with a population of only around 10,000 a great consolation destination.

Sedona is situated in a unique geographical area called the Mogollon Rim running across the State of Arizona. From the centre of the state it extends approximately 200 miles eastward from the mouth of the beautiful Oak Creek Canyon to near the border with New Mexico. It is this uniqueness of the landscape that makes people believe Sedona has some kind of "mystical powers".

Much of the land south of the Mogollon Rim lies 4,000 to 5,000 feet above sea level characterized by high limestone and sandstone cliffs called Kaibab Limestone and Coconino Sandstone. With this elevation in mind, don't get caught out with the weather.

When I arrived in early Spring I was greeted with bright, warm sunshine. When I woke up the next morning it was covered in 4 feet of snow!

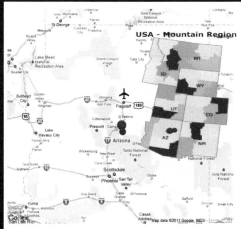

Sedona's Mogollon Rim is on the south western end of the vast Colorado Plateau, which extends into five other States.

The famous red rocks of Sedona are formed by a layer of rock known as the Schnebly Hill Formation. The Schnebly Hill Formation is a thick layer of red to orange coloured sandstone found only in the Sedona vicinity.

Also unique to the area and shooting up like giant green rockets is the worlds largest contiguous stand of Ponderosa Pine Trees. Making the scenery around Sedona pretty special.

# Sedona, Arizona

It was once thought that this whole area used to be under water and part of the Pacific Ocean during the Permian Period around 200 million years ago.

These ancient deposits of lime, mud and sandstone is what gives the rocks its uniqueness and variation in the colours due to thousands of years of erosion.

Sedona was named after Sedona Arabelle Miller Schnebly in the late 1800s. Sedona, was the wife of the city's first postmaster, Carl Schnebly.

Carl and Sedona where the first pioneers to arrive and built a large wooden home to accommodate guests and visitors who where passing-by.

The Schnebly brothers were obviously romantics at heart because they had a tendency to name things after their loved ones. His brother suggested the Post Office be named after Dona, in honour of his wife. Dona later became Sedona's nickname.

On arrival in Sedona the first challenge is finding somewhere to park. So try to get accommodation close to downtown, or drive down the back streets to find a space.

Just like Niagara Falls, I would highly recommend taking note of what your 'first impression' of Sedona is. It is this first impression that will stay with you long after you have left.

For me, it was the lush green valleys surrounded by huge multi-coloured rock formations as a panoramic backdrop. It has a similar "Wow" factor as Monument Valley, the Grand Canyon or Zion in Utah.

The downtown area is one long strip about a mile long full of shops, restaurants and tour operators offering various suggestions on how to sample the best of Sedona.

I would suggest booking yourself on the various tours first (they get booked up quite quickly) leaving you time to kill eating or purchasing souvenirs.

I booked the fast-food sounding Scenic Rim Combo and Coyote Canyon with Pink Jeep Tours.

You can hike, quad, bike or drive your own car around Sedona. But if you don't have a 4X4 or know the area, I wouldn't recommend it. Like white water rafting down the Grand Canyon this is one you enjoy with the experts!

So my tour began and I was taken in an open top florescent pink jeep. Up a few thousand feet along rugged trails to see the rock formations "up close and personal". Which engulf you the further up the trail you go.

On a good day (check the weather the day before) the scenery is magnificent and definitely worth the bouncy ride.

# Sedona, Arizona

Your guide explains the rock formations and the folk-lore names they have been christened with over the years. Names like Courthouse, Cathedral, Bell, Coffee-pot and Snoopy. I'm happy to report that the rock "Gaga" isn't represented yet!

Sedona has got a reputation as appealing to the hippie in you. People come here looking for spiritualism, readings, prayer, mystical to dark arts and all kinds of healing therapy from Chakra to Aura. There is even a Center for the New Age. Services offered are UFO Researcher and Investigator and Grandmother Wisdom Keeper. I picked some of my more favourite tag-lines from the various pamphlets designed to (amuse!) I mean entice you :

*"Connect with the Energy of Mother Earth, Through Ceremonial Cleansing of your Aura. Get your, Issues out of your Tissues. Connect with your Angels and Guides."*

*"Radiate the blessings of the American born Incarnation of Buddha Maitreya to Awaken the Soul/Buddha Nature. Divine essence within all beings".*

I might sound cynical, but I did meet two ladies who were into this kind of thing and attending a large organized weekend event. It turned out being involved in any kind of spiritualism in America is quite brave. Questioning the "bible-belt" majority in your local community is verging on witchcraft!

From my brief discussions with them they had got an awful lot of solace from these types of events. Good for them, I say.

I decided to embrace everything Sedona had to offer with an open mind. Starting with a guided Sedona Vortex tour.

Here we hiked at a leisurely pace to an area famed for where two Vortices meet. There are at least 5 known Vortex areas in Sedona, our guide described them as "spiralling, spiritual energy". Officially a vortex is a spinning rotation of energy often fluid or air, an example being the cone of a tornado.

So it is at this convergence of energies that the ceremony takes place, with crystals, stones and readings, designed to maximize the energy in the space.

The desired outcome being to cleanse your aura, balance out your chakras and remove unwanted blocks or disharmony. Stop laughing!

# $S$ *is for......*

# $S$edona

Personally I thought it was all pretty 'cool'. I think you get carried away in the moment, because you feel like you are doing something a bit "odd" and "different".

Not sure if my aura was cleansed or my chakras had been sorted out! But I certainly had a good "poo" that evening!!

All joking apart, it was quite an up-lifting experience.

As if to reaffirm their legitimacy, a number of people decide to get married at one of these kinds of sights or come in search of healing if they are feeling unwell.

If you have the time and have an open mind I would certainly recommend doing one of these guided Vortex trails.

My other recommendation would be to go and see the Chapel of the Holy Cross, near the vortex called Chicken Point.

Jutting out of the rock is the Chapel, built inside a thousand foot wall of rock. With a twin pinnacle 250ft spire sticking out of the mountain like a giant space-ship.

Purposely emptied of any religious symbols inside, it is designed to welcome people of all faiths and beliefs who come and sit in the space and take in the amazing view or perform their own personal spiritual act.

Although it can be busy the splendid architecture and fantastic views in every direction for miles around were crowd beating.

VOTED FOR BY THE AUTHOR

BEST IN AMERICA

Spiritual Destination

Sedona, Arizona

Another crowd puller in July is the National Day of the America Cowboy Celebration.

This event honours Arizona's western past with gun slinging, whip cracking cowboys performing attractions all day and into the night on Main Street Sedona.

If you are staying a few days and have exhausted the shopping in downtown Sedona, you may enjoy a trip out to the village of Oak Creek. It also has more fine arts, metaphysical stores and restaurants, but is less touristy.

On a similar vain, my final recommendation would be to take a trip down Route 179 and visit the Spanish-Colonial style Tlaquepaque

Arts & Crafts Village. It features high-end shops, galleries and a quaint chapel and creek.

On the way there I came across Tuzigoot National Monument. Near Cottonwood, it is one of the best Native American exhibits I came across in America.

So in summary, Sedona is a great little place to visit with plenty to do and fantastic scenery from the second you arrive.

As many of them are unique to Sedona, I would recommend booking any of the "alternative" activities before arriving to prevent disappointment.

From my travels across America, Sedona was unique and certainly wins my personal vote for the most spiritual and energizing place I was lucky enough to uncover.

# IF YOU HAVE MORE TIME ...

## Outdoors People

Visit the 1.8 million acre Coconino National Forest, with its seven wilderness areas, which encompasses the city of Sedona at altitudes from 3 to 12 thousand feet. This vast and scenic woodland features magnificent Ponderosa pines, lakes, spectacular canyons, snowcapped pinnacles and abundant wildlife. The woodlands also offer every type of recreational activity as well as the opportunity to visit archaeological sites. Check out: www.redrockcountry.org.

There is an extensive list of recreational activities and state parks. Many companies offer day hiking, horseback riding or bouncing around in a jeep on the trails that lead into the picturesque canyon. Book beforehand to prevent disappointment.

## History, Culture & Gifts

Like Santa Fe, Sedona is known as an Arts Mecca stemming back to the opening of the Sedona Arts Center in 1958. With the creation of the Cowboy Artists of America (CAA), the most successful art organization in American history. Nowadays it showcases the work of promising local artists for that uniquely Sedona gift.

Earth Day Celebration - April - Sedona recognizes its own beauty by honoring the planet with a full day of eco-friendly festivities at Posse Grounds Park. Featuring live entertainment, kids activities and organic foods from sustainable local vendors. Check out www.sedonaaz.gov.

## Photographers (People & Places)

Go to Sedona in late summer when the humidity creates terrific thunderstorms that crack against the rock formation sky-line to dramatic effect for budding photographers.

Or Head to Strawberry and Milk Ranch Point or other high points along the Mogollon Rim at sunset, on clear days you can see for over 50 miles in every direction. It's a stunning array of colours against the landscape and rock formations.

The Red Rock Scenic Byway is a 7.5 mile gateway, exit at No.298 off Interstate 17 where the route begins. The road winds through Coconino National Forest and the famous vortex sites.

## Only in America.....

Jump on the Verde Canyon Railway for a pristine ride through this wilderness area and look out for the canyon's resident bald eagle couple Black and Decker. You can get information here : www.verdecanyonrr.com.

More than 90 feature films (especially Westerns) and countless commercials have been shot in the Greater Sedona area. Streets there are named after them like *Johnny Guitar*, *Pony Soldier*, and *Gun Fury*. Stars who worked in Sedona include Humphrey Bogart, Elvis Presley, Johnny Depp, Robert DeNiro, Henry Fonda, Rock Hudson and hundreds of others.

# USA VOTED - TOP 6 'OTHER' LETTER "S" DESTINATIONS ...

### Santa Monica, California
Distance to Los Angeles International Airport is 12 miles or approx. 21mins.

### Salem, Massachusetts
Distance to General Edward Lawrence Logan International Airport is 14 miles or 30mins.

### Springfield, Illinois
Distance to Abraham Lincoln Capital Airport is 6 miles or 15mins.

### SeaWorld, Florida
Distance to Orlando International Airport is 13 miles or approx. 24mins.

### San Juan Island, Washington
Distance to Roche Harbor Airport is 9 miles or approx. 19mins.

### St. Augustine, Florida
Distance to Jacksonville International Airport is 58 miles or 1hr 11mins.

# $T$ _is for......_ $T$ ybee

**Tybee Island, Georgia -** Tiny Tybee is a warm summer destination surrounded by marshland beside a coastal inlet. So you can enjoy historic Savannah in the morning and be at the beach by the afternoon to watch the sunset.

"T" is for Tybee Island in Georgia. Tybee was first named by the Native Americans as their word for Salt. This small barrier island on the north east tip of the Georgia coast is a beautiful little place away from the sprawl of the big cities. Not far from beautiful Savannah it is a little gem of a place with beautiful white sandy beaches, coastal wetlands and marshy inlets.

It is not as well-known as some of the other island and coastal inlets (like Galveston, Texas, Mississippi Delta or Outer Banks, North Carolina etc). Which means it has managed to keep its small town, laid-back feel. But there is still plenty to do for all the family, you could easily stay a week or 2 weeks and take in all the recreational activities.

Just like its neighbour Savannah, Tybee has an interesting past. In 1855 a Fort was built and named in honour of General James Screven, a Revolutionary War hero. Fort Screven on the north end of Tybee was designed to provide a modern seacoast defence.

From 1897 to 1947, the fort was an integral part of America's Coastal Defence system. Troops even stood guard on Tybee through the Spanish American War of 1898 then World War I and World War II. As a visitor attraction its not that impressive, more bomb shelter than fort. So I would check out its neighbour instead, 10 minutes down the road at Fort Pulaski, now that's what you call a Fort!

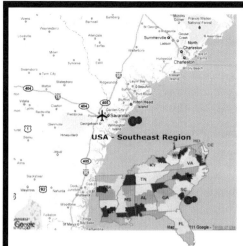

USA - Southeast Region

Fort Pulaski has stood guard over the Savannah River for over 150 years. Many of the defining events of Fort Pulaski occurred during the American Civil War. So its battle scars only add to the attraction.

It is an amazingly restored building and it is not very often you get to see a moat filled with water.

Other historical markers on Tybee are the Tybee Island Lighthouse or the Cockspur Island Lighthouse marking the South Channel of the Savannah River.

I am amused by how many Americans; like Europe, share a fascination with lighthouses.

# Tybee Island, Georgia

For me it comes under the same category as Train or Plane Spotting! But they are both quite impressive if you like lighthouses. Cockspur is much smaller and out on the wetlands, whereas Tybee has out buildings and is in much better condition.

If it is history and culture you are looking for then Savannah is for you. Savannah received a significant amount of Votes from many people on my trip across America. Having spent quite a while there I can totally see why.

It offers an eclectic mix of American-European architecture to rival London, Barcelona or Florence. Its interesting history and culture makes you feel like you have stepped back in time.

I got an all-day personal tour of Savannah by a generational resident Jill who took me to all the sites of the city. Including the church the feather falls from at the start of Forest Gump and the bench he sits on the do the "Life is like a box of Chocolates..." speech.

Having done all the sites in downtown Savannah, to my surprise we headed to a cemetery out of town.

The Bonaventure Cemetery was developed on the historically-significant site of the Bonaventure Plantation. This peaceful setting rests on a scenic bluff of the Wilmington River, east of Savannah.

Becoming a public cemetery in 1907, this charming site has been a world famous tourist destination for more than 150 years. Due to the old tree-lined roadways, the unique cemetery sculpture, architecture and folklore associated with it. Not forgetting the many notable persons interred here.

Before visiting try to read the book or watch this film; Midnight in the Garden of Good and Evil. Not a great film, but a famous book by John Berendt and many of the scenes are set in this cemetery.

One of the best things about traveling around with a personal guide was that I got to sample things Georgia Style. Like salt water peanuts, these are whole peanuts boiled until soft then then left in a huge vat of salty water. Strangely nice in the stifling heat of Georgia.

Luckily there is no shortage of ice cold refreshments to wash down the super salty peanuts. A slushy was Jill's choice of refreshment which came in Huge, Enormous and Binormous! Talking of Slushes, I would also recommend popping into Wet Willes who serve them alcoholic.

The food everywhere in Savannah is amazing, my personal recommendation would be Alligator Soul which offered a great electric mix of foods from the bayou. The bar is a great alternative seating area if you are traveling alone.

# Tybee Island, Georgia

I had the company of Wendy and another Savannah resident who told me that living in Savannah was like a small village "everyone knows your business".

Needless to say the food and company was outstanding. I had Alligator and Fried Green Tomatoes. I had a strange Love, Hate relationship with Fried Green Tomatoes. I tried them many times all over America, so you would think that I "loved them". But to be honest I "hated them" it didn't matter which state, I just didn't get it, who wants to each an unripe tomato covered in batter!

I have skimmed over Savannah but it is "must-see" using the quieter and sedate Tybee Island as your base. There is a shuttle bus or you can get a pre-booked taxi for around $50.00 (parking in Savannah is a nightmare).

Tybee itself also offers some excellent restaurant choices, you could sample a different one each night.

Seafood and crab seems to be the regional specialty. The Crab Shack which serves seafood in a bucket is great if you have a large family to feed.

For something more intimate and adult I would recommend AJ's Dockside. Family owned and operated by Alan and Jackie. They also have great seafood served by a group of young, friendly staff, happy to earn some very extra money during the busy season.

My experience of all the food in Tybee was generally good, you just need to be patient if you have gone at a peak hour.

If camping I would recommend buying your own food and contemplating a BBQ. There are plenty of markets selling fresh food, fruit and vegetables. I made a new friend at Davis Produce (755 Us Highway 80 E) always busy, lovely people and selling excellent fresh produce.

One thing you cannot escape in Tybee is a constant humming sound. It is made by a bug found in the region called a Cicada. It is the male that sings his love song trying to attract females. They do this by contracting their tymbal muscle which buckles the membrane inward, producing a loud click. When it snaps back it clicks again.

As it is the loudest song known in the insect world you can't miss it. Just 1 Cicada registers over 100 decibels, equivalent to a jackhammer or speeding express train going by!

Spanish Moss drapes elegantly from the trees around the region, so you can imagine when thousands of these get together it is like a Cicada Rock Concert!

# *T is for......* Tybee Island

The good news is that Cicadas generally do not bite or sting humans. If one lands on you don't freak out; like a lady sat next to me at dinner did, knocking all the drinks flying. Just brush it off and act cool!

Having travelled all 50 states, most notably Alaska and Hawaii, I believe I know a thing or two about sunsets.

But I have to say the ones I witnessed daily in Tybee, over the marsh lands were spectacular.

The humid Georgia days and blazing hot sun bestow a canopy of colours across the sky as the sun cools below the horizon.

Quite randomly and as if to underline Tybee's "what nice people they are" credentials. Whilst I was sitting there admiring the view I met a local resident and photographer, Joseph Sheilds.

Being a local he is familiar with everything Tybee and often photographs the sunsets. Check out his work for a more personal view of Tybee. Josephsheildsphotography.com

He asked to take my picture, then we just chatted passing the time of day with polite conversation enjoying the sunset.

It is such a relief to see the sun set because the unrelenting tropical heat in Georgia can sometimes make you feel like you are melting.

To take advantage of this, as the late afternoon hazy clouds begin to form grab yourself a bottle of wine. Jump on your bike and make your way down to the marshes or coast.

The beach at Tybee sticks out right on the far edge of Georgia's eastern border. Its golden white sands, warm waters and pier provide the perfect spot for watching the sunset.

Or head to one of the many salt marshes. Chilling out watching the sun dip under the Tybee horizon. Welcoming the cool breezes as they lap off the lush green lowlands. Grab yourself a cold drink, and enjoy the views. Providing the perfect setting and the perfect way to end the day. With Georgia on Your Mind.

VOTED FOR BY THE AUTHOR

**BEST IN AMERICA**

*Alligator*

Alligator Soul, 114 Barnard St

Savannah, Georgia

# IF YOU HAVE MORE TIME ...

## Outdoors People

Tybee Island is the perfect destination for the outdoor enthusiast, and offers activities from fishing and kayaking to jet-skiing and parasailing. For more information check out Tybee Island Parasail, Sundial Charters and Tybee Islands Water Sports.

Visit the Little Tybee nature preserve and see more species of coastal Georgia wildlife than you're likely to see anywhere else.

Or take in bottlenose dolphins in their natural habitat while savoring the scenic views of the Old Cockspur Lighthouse, Fort Pulaski and Tybee's North Beach on a dolphin boat tour. Here are the ones I would do further research on: Sweet Lowland Tours, Tybee Turtle Tour and Captain Mike's Dolphin Tours.

## History, Culture & Gifts

Native Americans, using dugout canoes to navigate the waterways, hunted and camped in Georgia's coastal islands for thousands of years. The Euchee tribe likely inhabited the island in the years preceding the arrival of the first Spanish explorers in the 16th century.

In 1520, the Spanish laid claim to what is now Tybee Island and named it Los Bajos. After various wars through the 17th century the Sea Islands were depopulated, allowing the establishment of new English settlements such as the colony of Georgia. In 1733 English settlers led by James Oglethorpe settled on Tybee Island before eventually moving on to settle in Savannah.

## Photographers (People & Places)

Worth a visit is the Tybee Island Light Station as it is one of just a handful of 18th century lighthouses still in operation in North America.

Every year since 1987 Tybee Island has had an annual Beach Bum parade, traditionally held in May. The parade route comes down the main road, Butler Avenue. As the parade floats goes-by onlookers have been known to shoot each other with water-guns.

Labor Day Beach Bash - enjoy the ocean breezes with live music filling the air from the Tybee Island Pier & Pavilion. Each year Tybee holds its Labor Day Beach Bash featuring free live entertainment & fireworks at the oceanfront. Check out: www.tybeefest.com

## Only in America.....

In the Fall, swashbucklers of all ages converge on Tybee Island to participate in the Annual Tybee Island Pirate Fest! Featuring a Pirate Victory Parade, live entertainment, costume contests and the Thieves Market filled with treasures, grog and grub! Arr!

In Feb 1958, a U.S. Air Force B-47 from Florida jettisoned a nuclear weapon off the coast of Tybee Island while conducting training exercises with a F-86. The two aircraft collided, the fighter pilot ejected and the bomber crew made an emergency landing. The lost weapon, the "Tybee Bomb" is still missing to this day! Yikes!

Hartsfield-Jackson Atlanta International Airport is the world's busiest airport, 10 miles south of downtown Atlanta, Georgia's capital city.

# USA VOTED - TOP 6 'OTHER' LETTER "T" DESTINATIONS ...

**The 4 Corners, UT, NM, AZ, CO**
Distance to Cortez-Montezuma County Airport is 38 miles or approx. 47mins.

**Tahoe City, California**
Distance to Sacramento International Airport is 121 miles or 2hrs 11mins.

**Tacoma, Washington**
Distance to Seattle-Tacoma International Airport is 30 miles or 35mins.

**Times Square, New York**
Distance to LaGuardia Airport is 9 miles or approx. 23mins.

**Toledo, Ohio**
Distance to Detroit Metropolitan Wayne County Airport is 56 miles or approx. 1hr 6mins.

**Taos, New Mexico**
Distance to Taos Regional Airport is 9 miles or 12mins.

# *U* is for...... U niversity of...

# MICHIGAN
### THE BIG HOUSE AT ANN ARBOR

**University of Michigan and Michigan State, Michigan** - Welcome to The Big House

the biggest game in American College Football. With 110,000 plus fans in attendance,

let the tailgating begin.

"U" is for the University of ___ ?? On my travels across America so many people wanted to Vote for their College, High School , Elementary School or University. So in honour of all those people I decided not to ignore the importance of these institutions in American life and let-one -in the book.

Now I am sorry to announce to all the Notre Dame, LSU, Buckeye, Ole Miss, Alabama and all the other football fans. That the runaway winner was the biggest game in the football college calendar, The University of Michigan versus Michigan State University Game at The Big House.

As an American football (what we call it in Europe) novice and bearing in mind "I am a girl", I will attempt to explain roughly how the game works. I apologize up-front to all the Americans I have met on my travels who will be giggling at my explanation.

So there are two teams made up of 11 players, one team is attacking (offense) and the other team is defending (D-fence). However there can be as many as 53 "hanger-onners" and as many as 45 of these may play in each game.

This is in comparison to the 15 players on a Rugby team and 7 substitutes! I will let you make -up your own inappropriate "girlie wimp jokes here!"

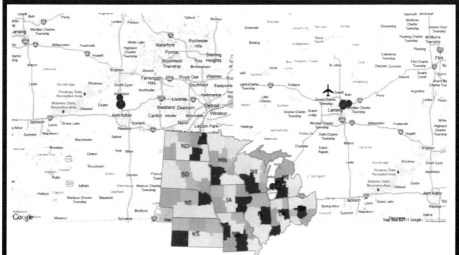

**USA - Midwest Region**

# Universities of Michigan

The attacking (offense) team has four attempts; called Downs, at trying to get the ball 10 yards. They have various pre-planned offensive moves or Plays to do this.

Failure to get the 10 yards normally results in a walloping kick right down the other end of the pitch (or field). So the other team can have their turn yards down the field.

Or you could have a Turnover when the other team is able to grab the ball, then the offensive and defense switch rolls. Whoever has scored the most points at the end of 4 quarters (15mins each) is the winner. Simples!

So when you hear the commentator say "3rd down and 6 to go". It basically means, it is the 3rd chance and they have 6 yards to gain. A bit like 6th tackle in Rugby League.

There are lots of other things I could bore you with, but for all intents and purposes that's all you need to know.

Michigan State University (MSU), (guys in green) is in East Lansing, Michigan. Founded in 1855, it was the pioneer land-grant institution and served as a model for future land-grant colleges in the United States under the 1862 Morrill Act. What this means in "English terms" is that it has an agricultural bias or is a Sheep Shagging University!

It is for this reason that is the University of Michigan (guys in blue) perceives itself as more superior than MSU. Or so I was told by both sides!

But if you look at the facts, this is actually not true. MSU pioneered the studies of packaging, hospitality business, telecommunication and music therapy. Today its study-abroad program is the largest in the country, offering more than 200 programs in more than 60 countries on all continents including Antarctica.

After World War II, the number of students tripled as the institution became a major university. It is considered to be one of America's Public Ivy universities, which recognizes top public research universities.

Today, MSU is the ninth-largest university in the United States, with over 47 thousand students and 2 thousand plus faculty members. Sports at both Universities is like religion with MSU's known as the Spartans.

The other guys, The University of Michigan is about an hour away in Ann Arbor, Michigan. It is the state's oldest university founded in 1817 in Detroit.

Since its establishment the university has expanded to include more than 584 major buildings and transformed its academic program from a strictly classical curriculum to one that includes science and research.

# Universities of Michigan

In 1995 it was ranked third nationally for the quality of its graduate programs. Michigan has one of the world's largest living alumni groups with 460,000 people.

"The Big House" which is the main stadium of The Wolverines is the largest American football stadium in the world.

The Big House is also affectionally known as "Jail" in American society. I wondered why I was getting funny looks when I told people out of state I was going "to the big house!"

University of Michigan colours are maize (yellow) and blue (navy), not be to mistaken for the green and white that the State of Michigan University wear. Yes, I know that is confusing, I proceeded to get it wrong all day long!

In honour of the occasion I had dyed my Mohawk blue and yellow, and wore green and white in order to look neutral. Having attended numerous soccer/football games in my time I know being neutral can sometimes prevent you from injury!

If the hype is true then the university town swells by almost 300,000 on the weekends of the rivalry game. The stadium itself has a capacity of 107,000 people not to mention the hundreds and thousands of RVs and tailgaters that cram into any spare space in and around the stadium and nearby streets.

Tickets for the game become more valuable than gold as game time approached.

I was lucky enough to meet some people in Mackinac Island who worked for Comcast who happened to be the main sponsor of the game. They invited me along as their VIP.

Eventually I did find them, but decided to ditch them as they were 'too corporate' in their suits, talking business. My PTSD symptoms always started to bubble when I was around business people in suits, so I made a sharp exit.

So using my politest English accent I managed to crash a Michigan tailgating party and met a group of very welcoming people.

To set the scene, there were at least four families and around 200 people. They had got up super early the day before, got their RVs and trucks and driven to their pre-booked spaces to save them.

# U is for......

# University of...

They had then spent the next 48 hours getting ready for the upcoming festivities. They had gazebos, tables and chairs and 4 huge fridges stacked with cold beer, wines and spirits. They had even brought toilets!

Not to mention of course, numerous satellite televisions dotted around their spot. God bless America!

I was grateful to spend the afternoon with them all.

Then as game time got nearer I made my way towards the stadium.

VOTED FOR BY THE AUTHOR

BEST IN AMERICA

Tailgating
The Big House, Ann Arbor
Michigan

Once inside the magnitude of the experience comes over you in waves. This was Americana at its very best. The band's, cheerleaders, colours, the food and the constant "whooping". It was just as I had hoped it would be, "Go Blue, Go Green!"

In honour of my experience I made a short video. You can check it out on You-Tube: A to Zee Across America – Michigan -- The Big House.

So after the National Anthem and lots of cap taking-off the game started. The general feeling I had got from spending time with both sets of fans, was that Michigan State were considered the under-dogs. So it was to everyone's surprise that the first team to score was in fact Michigan State. Go Green!

Then again and again. Surely not, the Wolverines cannot be playing this badly? Hilariously the Spartans fan in front of me celebrated every point by mimicking a pole dancer!

With snake-like dancing and pouting pretending to twirl his nipples. I think he was hammered!

I have to be honest and say that watching the game at field side is actually quite tricky because the plays occur so fast and unlike TV you don't have the advantage of an instant replay. I was beginning to understand why many of the tail-gators simply stayed in the parking lot and watched the game on TV.

The atmosphere inside the stadium was immense. Especially when the student bodies broke into their team's Fight Songs. Something about "We're going to win this game, Fight! Fight! Rah Fight! Victory for MSU!"

Then there was the half-time show, or whatever its called? This was the best bit for me. I had no idea this was going to happen.

On came the Universities Marching Bands and Cheerleaders. First the visiting teams then the home team. Well this was great, 50 to 100 people clanging glockenspiels, drums and throwing each other up in the air. I thought this was just something Hollywood had dreamt up, but here it was to my viewing surprise.

I have to admit it was a tad bit "camp", but they all seemed to be enjoying it, especially the boys. Kurt Hummel eat your heart out! Serous stuff this cheerleading malarkey, some universities even offer scholarships!

Then back to the game for the 3rd quarter, at last Michigan University did start to come back into it.

Fast forward and it turned-out I should have dyed my hair green and white because the under-dogs Michigan State University won. Doh!

Eventually I made my way out of the stadium and after wandering around for ages I found my new buddies back at the tailgate party.

When I got there the fans of the under-dog Spartan's, who had taken significant stick before the game, were jubilant.

Of course, even more food and beer was being wheeled in for the post-match celebrations. Whilst everyone crammed in front of the TV to debate the game.

# Universities of Michigan

One of the lady's sons was a player for the University of Michigan and I was lucky enough to meet him. Unsurprisingly, he was huge!

The night wore on with more beers then out came the Shuffled Board. Yey. I first came across this game in Alabama. The objective is to throw a bean bag around 50 yards onto a tilted wooden board and into the hand sized hole.

It is surprisingly addictive, caution though most American's are highly competitive and take it really seriously. Chest bumps, high fives, bitch comments. You can imagine!

What a great day out and huge thanks to all those people I met randomly at the tail-gate. Thanks for making me feel so welcome and happily sharing. Should you ever find yourself heading to Old Trafford or the Nou Camp I'll happily return the favour.

I decided to make my way back to the hotel, walking was the only option. This too turned into an adventure, I came across lots of student houses. Not being shy, I decided I would gate crash these too.

I found myself in what I guess you would call a "frat house" (ala) Animal House. I went in and made myself welcome, as it was something o'clock at this point things seemed to be winding down a bit from what had obviously been one hell of a party. Toga, Toga!

I got talking to some of the students who where at the University of Michigan.

They were telling me how competitive it is to get into and how much it all costs. Out of state students pay around $33,000 a year for tuition and board.

I can confirm Frat Houses Rock, needless to say, I finally got to my hotel room as the sun was coming up.

If you are from Europe, Oz, Asia or Africa then I would strongly recommend you go and see an America sport. It is a truly unique experience compared to our cultures, I felt honoured to have experienced it.

This was not the first nor the last football game I went to across America. I saw many truly American sports whilst I was there and always really enjoyed them, but nothing ever compared to "The Big House".

Go Green!

## IF YOU HAVE MORE TIME ...

### History, Culture & Gifts

#### Michigan State University

The Michigan Constitution of 1850 called for the creation of an "agricultural school" so in 1855 Michigan Governor Kinsley S. Bingham signed a bill establishing the United States' first agriculture college the Agricultural College of the State of Michigan. So Michigan State University (MSU) was born and classes began in 1857. The college first admitted women in 1870, although at that time there were no female residence halls. The course was called "Women Course" and was home economics based.

By 1925 it was growing and had changed its name to Michigan State College of Agriculture and Applied Science (M.S.C.). With the help of the 1945 G.I. Bill, World War II veterans became the main stayers. From 1964 onwards the institution started to go by the name of Michigan State University.

In 2006 Michigan State, the University of Michigan and Wayne State University created the University Research Corridor. This alliance was formed to transform and strengthen Michigan's economy by reaching out to businesses, policymakers, investors and the public to speed up technology transfer and help attract new jobs to the state. Which was just in-time for the economic downturn of the car industry, the main employer in the State.

In 2007, Michigan State University established an education center in Dubai, MSU Dubai. It was the first American university with a presence in the UAE with classes beginning in August 2008.

Today MSU has over 200 academic programs with 17 degree granting colleges.

#### The University of Michigan

University of Michigan became a favored choice for bright Jewish students from New York in the 1920s and 1930s when the Ivy League schools had quotas restricting the number of Jews that could be admitted. As a result, UM gained the nickname "Harvard of the West".

It is no surprise to find out that fraternities and sororities play a major role in the university's social life; approximately 18 percent of undergraduates are involved in Greek life. Four different Greek councils exist with over 3,000 members making it one of the largest in the nation.
......"This Greek business. What's that all about?!"

### Only in America.....

The MSU Fight Song is the official fight song of Michigan State University. MSU's fight song was created in early 1915 when MSU was known as Michigan Agricultural College (M.A.C.). An MSU cheerleader, Francis Irving Lankey with Arthur Sayles created the song by combining original lyrics with the melody from an early 20th-century hymn called "Stand Up, Stand Up For Jesus".

The University of Michigan's fight song, The Victors, was written by student Louis Elbel in 1898 following the last-minute football victory over the University of Chicago that won them a league championship. The song was declared by John Philip Sousa (a famous American composer) as "the greatest college fight song ever written." The song refers to the university as being The Champions of the West.

# USA VOTED - TOP 6 'OTHER' LETTER "U" DESTINATIONS ...

### Union City, New Jersey
Distance to LaGuardia Airport is 21 miles or approx. 32mins.

### Upper East & West Side, New York City
Distance to LaGuardia Airport is 9 miles or approx. 19mins.

### Upper Peninsula, Michigan
Distance to MBS International Airport is 30 miles or approx. 1hr 54mins.

### Utica, New York State
Distance to Griffiss International Airport is 16 miles or approx. 27mins.

### Universal Studios, California
Distance to Bob Hope International Airport is 6 miles or approx. 16mins.

### Ukiah, California
Distance to Sacramento International Airport is 137 miles or approx. 2hrs 28mins.

# V is for......

# Venice Beach

**Venice Beach, California -** Instantly recognizable from all the TV shows and movies its been in. Fantastic beach, bizarre shops selling everything and anything. Dare you to look behind the Hollywood façade? Its called Tinsel Town for a reason!

"V" is for Venice Beach, California. This is an area I am very familiar with for a number of happy and sad reasons. This is where my husband (Ozzy John) and I lived when we first arrived in California in 2007. Sadly it is just off Venice Beach in the Pacific Ocean on a sailing trip that John had died in my arms, ever since then I had become afraid of the water and couldn't bare to watch the sunset dipping under the Pacific.

All our friends and family who visited always liked Venice Beach, being a resident you could see through the façade. I still have found memories of it, John had spent time here with his parents in the spring and we had spent Christmas Day with my family. Venice Beach was also where we went 2 years after his death and sold his photographs for charity on the boardwalk. But for me, Venice Beach is the place me and John walked every Sunday to have breakfast.

Having run away from that life and left all that behind, it seemed ironic that America would Vote for me to return to a place that fills me with such fear and dread. But "Having come this far I couldn't turn round now", I thought to myself.

Venice Beach is instantly recognizable because you will have seen it on countless TV, movie, adverts and magazines. You find yourself walking down the crowded boardwalk with a wide variety of weird and wonderful vendors either side wanting to sell you anything from souvenirs, food, slogan T-shirts, creative arts to marijuana paraphernalia.

It is a circus on the senses and bizarrely against the back drop of multi-million dollar homes. It has the best "people-watching" of anywhere in the US. Beautiful bodies, golden beaches, basketball, muscles and hand-bag dogs all draped in the year-round Californian sunshine.

Check out this video on You Tube: Lucozade Advert — Louder—DJ Fresh ft Sian Evans and you'll get the picture.

Venice Beach was originally founded by tobacco millionaire Abbot Kinney in 1905. By digging and draining several miles of canals and marshes for his residential area.

# Venice Beach, California

He built a 1,200-foot long pleasure pier with an auditorium, ship restaurant, dance hall, hot salt-water plunge and a block-long arcade of shops with Venetian architecture.

With tourists mostly arriving on the Red Cars of the Pacific Electric Railway from Los Angeles and Santa Monica. You could then board Venice's miniature railroad and gondolas to tour the town.

But the biggest attraction was Venice's mile long gently sloping beach. With Cottages and housekeeping tents being available for rent.

Attractions on the Kinney Pier became more amusement-oriented by 1910, with an Aquarium, Virginia Reel, Whip, Racing Derby and game booths being added.

For the amusement of the public, Kinney hired aviators to do aerial stunts over the beach. One of them, movie aviator and Venice airport owner B.H. DeLay, implemented the first light plane airport in the United States on DeLay Field. Look out for DeLay Drive which runs from Venice Beach into LA.

By 1925, Venice's politics became unmanageable. Its roads, water and sewage systems badly needed repair and expansion to keep up with its growing population.

It was felt that the town needed more streets, not canals, so most of them were paved in during 1929 after a three-year court battle led by canal residents.

Los Angeles had neglected Venice for so long that by the 1950s, it had become the "Slum by the Sea." Low rents for run-down bungalows attracted predominantly European immigrants (a substantial number being Holocaust survivors). This became where the young counterculture artists, poets and writers lived.

The amusement park suffered a series of arson fires beginning in 1970 and demolished in 1974. The Aragon Ballroom and later the Cheetah Club where rock bands such as the Doors appeared was shut down in the 1960s.

Ironically those "Slum of the Sea" immigrants who have passed on their houses from generation to generation now have some of the most expensive real estate in the world.

Like it is for me 'personally' I find Venice Beach to be a mixed-up set of contradictions. Venice Beach symbolizes everything that is "Good" about America, whilst at the same time (if you are prepared to look) it will also show you everything that is "Bad" about America.

You can easily walk down Venice Beach and be amused by the fun T-shirts and weird looking people who pass by. Or dream of living in one of the multi-million dollar homes and looking like a million dollars.

But from my experience of travelling all 50 States, that is not "real" America.

# Venice Beach, California

Having met hundreds and hundreds of "real" Americans, Venice Beach is just a fantasy. There is a reason why Los Angeles is called Tinsel Town!

If you spend anytime at these "alleged" multimillion dollar homes you will realize that the canals are actually quite disgusting and smelly.

Go there at night and you will see the "real" Venice Beach with its crack-heads, alcoholics and hundreds of homeless people. In its torrid past Venice used to be a place for "the unclean" or "unwelcome". Today it still has that sense, especially if you go there at night. Welcome to California, glitteringly, superficial!

Bel-air, Beverly Hills, the Hollywood and Malibu Hills have a very screwed-up ideal when it comes to the distribution of wealth. Because less than 40 minutes away is Skid Row in downtown Los Angeles.

Skid Row is like a small town. It is about 20 blocks by 20 blocks during the day and swells at night. I "dare" anyone to spend 1 night there, it is one of the scariest experiences you will ever have. It is like a Real-Life War Zone in the middle of downtown Los Angeles. Ironically you can see the Hollywood sign from it! "Welcome to Hollywood! What's your dream? Everybody comes here; this is Hollywood, land of dreams!"

After John's death, 5 months later in the November, I was diagnosed with PTSD by my Doctor.

Due to ignorance and fear around mental illness I ended-up spending time in the company of these types of people. In fact when I was released a week or so later, the White Van (Seriously, I am not making this up!) Drove to Skid Row and dropped everyone off. If you find yourself accidentally driving through there you will get mobbed too.

I ended-up on Skid Row because a guy I met when locked-up Frankie (homeless and a heroine addict) asked for my help. There are hostels there that house and feed addicts, homeless and the destitute.

Whilst there I saw an elderly black lady get gang raped in the street and it was just normal. She was so "off her face" she didn't even know what was happening.

As shocking as that was, seeing middle class young families queuing to have some food and somewhere semi-safe to sleep was abhorrent.

Don't get me wrong I know there is abject poverty all across the world. But to see this happening minutes away from million-dollar residential areas was hard to understand.

For instance, Pretty Woman since its release in 1990 has grossed more than $463,406,268. Did you know at $20 a meal you could feed all of LA's homeless for around 3 years.

I too had bought into that dream briefly, but not anymore. "I'm alright Jack" is certainly not the way I have been raised. I don't sign-up to the Self-preservation Society.

That is why places like Venice Beach are such a contradiction for me and how traveling the rest of the United States gave me so much solace.

Luckily I was to find out that wasn't the way "real" American's thought. In fact the majority of the American's I met across the other 49 States hated California and everything it stood for. Many had left and had no intention of going back.

Don't get me wrong, I don't hate California, I think it is a great place to visit. The theme parks, San Diego, San Francisco, Yosemite, Big Bear, Nappa and the Redwood Forests when I visited were fantastic.

As for LA, you must visit it at least once. Santa Monica, Laguna Beach, Hollywood and Beverly Hills should definitely be on your tourist destinations.

If I was going this would be my list of "must-see" recommendations having lived there:

- Go to all the theme parks. Booking the VIP experience where you can.
- Take a shopping trip to The Grove, Century City or 3rd Street Promenade.
- BBQ in Korean Town.

- Watch something at the Hollywood Bowl or go see the Dodgers or Lakers.
- Eat at The Cheesecake Factory, Gordon Ramsey's LA or Tom Colicchio's - Craft restaurant.
- Go sailing off Marina Del Rey.
- Go clubbing on Sunset Boulevard.

If you want to shop, drive-everywhere, eat healthy, be plastic and enjoy the best weather in America then you should definitely come here. The Stuff of Movie Stars.

But my travel guide has been about giving you a feel for a place so you can decide for yourself whether you would like it.

So if you only have one place in America you could visit then I would give Los Angeles a miss. I would head down to San Diego, Huntington Beach or San Francisco instead. Or skip Southern California all together and head for the north of the State.

There are many other cities in America I would rate over LA. Nashville, New York, Boston, Chicago, Miami to name a few.

So that was Venice Beach, it was good whilst it lasted. Keep up the glitteringly superficial work. But just remember Skid Row doesn't appear on any tourist maps!

# IF YOU HAVE MORE TIME ...

## Outdoors People

A trip to Disneyland should definitely be on the list. Also book yourself to go VIP to Universal Studios it's alittle more expensive, but absolutely worth it. Go to Six Flags both the water park and the roller coaster part, all the rides are scary so not for small children.

Malibu Beach and Huntington Beach are much better beaches to surf on than some of the main beaches around Venice Beach.

If you have the time, take a trip to Catalina Island, it's a great place to go for lunch and an afternoon walk-around.

If you have the time and it's the right time of year head towards Big Bear or Lake Tahoe and go and do some ski-ing or boarding.

## History, Culture & Gifts

In Santa Monica 3rd Street Promenade is generally known as the best place to shop. There are 2 other malls within a 40 minute drive Century City and The Grove (which also has a Farmers Market) both of which have all the major department stores.

If you are looking to splash out there are numerous shops in and around Beverly Hills, but most are quite intimidating. Most people just walk up and down the famous Rodeo Drive and have their picture taken because there are no prices on anything and the security guards are quite off-putting.

## Photographers (People & Places)

From Santa Monica take the Pacific Coastal Highway round to Malibu then slowly make your way back again. At any of the major junctions turn away from the coast and go up into the mountains, again you will get some great shots at sunset.

Do some research about downtown Los Angeles, there are some fantastic art deco buildings that have recently been renovated and take a unique picture. An example is the Eastern Buildings, a newly renovated apartment buildings. Or for a nautical theme head to Marina Del Rey, the biggest Marina in the world.

Also try and see an event at the Hollywood Bowl, Lakers or Dodgers.

## Only in America ...

When you down to Venice Beach, look out for this guy. He's called Harry Perry (aka) Jimi Hendrix on Skates. He has been a street performer for over 30 years now. His performance is basically to skate up and down Venice beach whilst playing an electric guitar and smiling very broadly with his Californian teeth.

For celebrity spotting head to Paradise Cove, Malibu Lagoon or Brentwood.

Carroll Hall Shelby was one of America's premiere sports car drivers in the 60s until a heart condition ended his career. He decided to turn to race car manufacturing. In 1964, he opened his first Shelby manufacturing plant in Venice. Today these cars are incredibly sort after around the world.

# USA VOTED - TOP 6 'OTHER' LETTER "V" DESTINATIONS ...

**Vail, Colorado**
Distance from Denver International Airport is 144 miles or 2hrs 32mins.

**Vashon Island, Washington**
Distance to Sea-Tac International Airport to Hershey is 23 miles or approx. 1hr 5mins.

**Ventnor City, New Jersey**
Downtown to Atlantic City Municipal Airport is 3 miles or 9mins.

**Valdez, Alaska**
Distance to Ted Stevens Anchorage International Airport is 306 miles or approx. 5hrs 40mins.

**Vero Beach, Florida**
Distance to Palm Beach International Airport is 79 miles or 1hour 28mins.

**Vineyard Haven, Massachusetts**
Distance to T.F. Green Airport is 90 miles or 2hrs 7mins.

# *W is for......*

# White Mountains

> **White Mountains, New Hampshire -** The perfect location to enjoy the spectacular colours of New England in the Fall. A warm welcome awaits you in New Hampshire and why not try a Highland Fling!

"W" is for the White Mountains, New Hampshire. Many of you will have heard of New England in the Fall, now may I present to you New Hampshire in the Fall. Which is roughly within the same area, but the New Hampshire side is probably not as busy as the Massachusetts side.

The White Mountains are a mountain range covering about a quarter of the state of New Hampshire and a small portion of western Maine. Part of the Appalachian Mountains, they are considered the most rugged mountains in New England. The range is heavily visited due to its proximity to Boston and (to a lesser extent) New York City.

There has been much discussion about the origin of the name White Mountains. This name and similar ones such as White Hills or Wine Hills are found in literature from colonial times. So the name possibly originates from then, because the highest peaks would often be snowcapped. An alternate theory is that the mica-cover which forms on the granite surface of the summits often looks white to observers.

Whatever brings you here, it is a beautifully scenic area to find yourself in during early spring or in the fall to see the mosaic of the season. I found the people to be friendly offering a genuine warm welcome. It was one of the most under-rated, scenic and welcoming states I came across in the whole US.

Most of the area is public land, including the White Mountain National Forest as well as a number of State Parks.

Its most famous peak is Mount Washington, which at 6,288 feet is one of a line of summits called the Presidential Range. Named after US presidents and other prominent Americans.

In addition, the White Mountains include several smaller groups including the Franconia Range, Sandwich Range, Carter-Moriah Range, Kinsman Range and Pilot Range.

# White Mountains Region, New Hampshire

New Hampshire as a whole reminded me of many alpine destinations in Europe. You drive around mountain scenery interjected with the odd sleepy villages nestled inside deep green forests. (à la) Sound of Music.

The area in all, has forty-eight peaks over 4,000ft, affectionately known as the Four-Thousand Footers. In true New Hampshire welcoming style, they have a system of alpine huts set-up by the Appalachian Mountain Club for hikers to utilize.

I started my journey in north west New Hampshire following the White Mountain National Forest which eventually took me to Carroll and Bretton Woods.

I was lucky enough to stay at the opulent Grand Hotel - Mount Washington Resort. Made famous because it was the site of the United Nations Monetary and Financial Conference in 1944. The Bretton Woods name being given to the system that led to the establishment of both the World Bank and the International Monetary Fund in 1945.

If you get chance to stay here I would highly recommend it, its like staying at a museum. You imagine the pictures starring at you as you walk by.

On the subject of accommodation, you can imagine I have stayed is some really good and really bad places in America. Bretton Woods was a good one and reminded me a tad of The Stanley Hotel I had visited near Denver in Colorado.

This is the hotel they used in the film The Shining. I can confirm it is still as spooky. Most of the original features that appear in the film are still present in the hotel. As soon as you walk-in and are faced with the double staircase, you'll flashbacked to the film.

I felt my blood run cold! I didn't have the bottle to stay overnight in the end. "Red Rum, Red Rum!"

I mention this because I had a similar feeling when I went to Bretton Woods, especially seeing the hotel in the winter. From a similar era they both feature lavish wood interiors and have a look of the hotel in the film.

Heading away from Bretton Woods I decided to take the scenic route through the White Mountains National Forest.

I headed to Crawford Notch State Park to Barlett, Conway Lake. Circling back via Flume Gorge and Franconia State Park.

This is a really good way to see the whole area. Conway Lake and Diana's Bath Waterfalls were beautifully peaceful in an amazing woodland setting. Barlett looks like an alpine village you would see in a miniature village display of the Alps and the perfect stop-off for lunch.

You will see signs along the way for Flume Gorge with no indication as to what it is. I can confirm it is very tall waterfall, cut inside a gash in the rocks, with a stairway allowing you to climb to the top.

# White Mountains Region, New Hampshire

First stop on arrival to Franconia should be Echo Lake. Surrounded by vast mountains the lake has a trail that goes all the way around it. You can camp, hike or fish here in relative isolation.

As it was nearly winter when I visited, I decided to stay at a near-by hotel called the Mittersill Alpine. This too, turned out to be quite an experience for all the wrong reasons.

This one would probably come under the heading of bad accommodation. Don't get me wrong, this is an alpine lodge in a beautiful setting, but inside it was like a labyrinth.

It was a maze of corridors, random rooms and dead ends with no clear numbering system. Full of what looked like care home lounges, old arcade games and the odd room filled with just mirrors. I kept stumbling outside into bricked-in courtyards and setting door alarms off.

As the hotel was empty, when I arrived the 80 year-old owner had given me the Honeymoon Suite. I had a sunken bath, four poster-bed, entertaining area, his and her bath robes! Eventually after about an hour of wandering around aimlessly, I found my suite.

That night I had a fantastic night out at a local pub just down the road with the very English sounding name of The Horse and Hound Inn. Having explained why I was there, the landlord Kerry and Kerrie (so that was easy) proceeded to introduce me to everyone as the token English person.

After numerous drinks and stories, out came the Franconia Alpine Ski Shot tradition. This involved putting about 10 shot glasses on an extra long wooden alpine ski. Then 10 people standing in a row downed their shots to a countdown from the locals and the ringing of alpine cow bells!

My recollection of the evening became alittle sketchy the more of these Alpine Ski Shots we consumed.

I do remember though in great detail meeting a group of muscle-clad Navy Seals who had just completed a training exercise in the nearby mountains and had come into the pub for last orders.

Them, not knowing about me recently becoming widowed, couldn't understand why I didn't find them the most utterly attractive men on the planet!

This competitive, testosterone driven immaturity soon turned into a drinking competition refereed by one of the Carrey's. American's are not known for their high alcohol tolerance. So I am proud to report for all the "sisters" out there that I successfully drank all five Navy Seals under the table. Who-rar!

Little did I know though that my greatest challenge would lie ahead at the Mittersill Alpine Resort in trying to find my room!

# White Mountains Region, New Hampshire

I swear it took me about two hours. By accident I had left my video camera on and there is hour after hour of me wander around in circles, letting door alarms off!

I must have had an alcohol induced sleep because I woke up fully clothed in the empty sunken bath! — "yes, I had made it!"

The next morning to my utter surprise and delight I found out that in the next county they were holding their Annual Highland Games. Being English and having married an Australian/Scotsman I thought I should go and look-up our Clan in America.

What better way to get over a hangover than to endure the painful sound of bag-pipes and a huge bowl of sheep stomach (Haggis). Mmm, yummy!

This was great fun, I parked-up "Reggie the RV" and jumped on a big yellow high school bus, which was a new experience for me. I was taken down to Lincoln, New Hampshire and the Loon Mountain Highland Games.

Having lived in Scotland for a while I had been to the Highland Games, so I was certainly looking forward to feeling the warmth of home 4,000 miles away.

It did not disappoint, the first thing I found was a stall selling "UK" items.

This is a strange phenomenon if you have never lived in a different country. It is strange the things that remind you of "Home" and that you miss.

You would expect in today's global economies that you could pretty much get everything, anywhere. But this is not always the case. For example, Dairy Milk chocolate in the UK tastes different to Dairy Milk in the USA (apparently something to do with the restrictions on milk content).

Unsurprisingly Tea in the UK is like a Religion with many different types. Unlike America when you are generally only offered breakfast tea. We also have drinks Americans have never even heard of like Vimto, Tizer and Lucozade.

So to be seeing all these delicacies all in one place was like an addiction craving! I nearly bought the whole store. I don't even like tea!

I said "...Ock.. I.." to the American Robertson Clan and the usual obligatory Scottish purchase of your Clan's tartan. Then it was time for Hangover Food and nothing says Scotland better that a Scotch Egg, Haggis, Neeps and Tatties.

# W *is for......*

# W hite Mountains

For the Americans reading this, you'll need to Google all this. Trying to explain the whole traditions of the Scottish and their foods in one paragraph just isn't going to cut it!

Then I sat there with my "wee dram" watching the marching bands with their bag pipes and brightly coloured tartans reminiscing about my time in Scotland.

Like the time I was beaten up by a group of girls for being English in the toilet in Ayr at Hogmanay. Or the fact that I was playfully called "The English Bas**ard" the whole time I was there by the Scots. Oh happy days!

VOTED FOR BY THE AUTHOR
BEST IN AMERICA
Loon Mountain, Scottish Food
White Mountains, Highland Games
New Hampshire

Seriously though the Highland Games in New Hampshire was very well organized and if you are in the area at the time I would certainly recommend you pay it a visit.

So taken with this whole area I spent quite a few nights under the stars at Echo Lake and Franconia Notch State Park surrounded by Cannon Mountain and The Flume.

If you like camping then this is the perfect spot. I went hiking, fishing and hunting here with some success. It is easy to get lost in the wilderness of New Hampshire and the more isolated you become the more you appreciate the region.

If you have ever fancied seeing New England in the Fall and you are doing it unguided.

Then here are my recommendations of regions to head to: Cape Cod, The Berkshires and Boston in Massachusetts.

Onto The White Mountains in New Hampshire. Cape Elizabeth and Bar Harbor, Maine. Then Newport, Rhode Island, Mystic in Connecticut and the Champlain Valley, Vermont.

There are lots of places to visit inside these regions, but generally speaking if you hit these areas who can't go far wrong.

Make sure you don't come to late though and miss the foliage change. As many are also famed as an excellent winter snow destination.

I visited New Hampshire just before the big snows, when the nights were becoming colder and the effects of fall were in full affect. Surrounded by such a beautiful landscape it is hard not to fall in love with it.

It is also less popular than the traditional Massachusetts Fall destinations meaning you can dodge the retired coach parties coming down from Canada.

Everywhere I went the people were all so welcoming and lovely. They had a laid-back charm which immediately put you at ease.

If you want to see America in its full glory, then I don't think you could find a much better place to visit that the White Mountains of New Hampshire.

# IF YOU HAVE MORE TIME ...

## Outdoors People
On Cannon Mountain there is a natural feature dubbed The Basin at Coney Lake. Consisting of a granite bowl, 20 feet in diameter, fed by a waterfall and worn smooth by the Pemigewasset River. The Basin is a popular spot for swimming in the ice-cold mountain-fed water. In fact this whole area around Canon Mountain is great for hiking in the summer and is famous for its winter pursuits.

New Hampshire has many State Parks with some 800,000 acres in The White Mountain National forest alone. Head to Crawford Notch for 6 miles of unspoiled rugged natural beauty, ideal for hiking, fishing or photography. Franconia Notch State Park is a deep valley with over 6,000 acres of woodland between the towering peaks of the Franconia and Kinsman Mountain ranges along the trails of the Appellations.

## History, Culture & Gifts
The White Mountains are part of the larger New England In The Fall province, which in turn is part of the larger Appalachians Mountain Range. The magma intrusions forming the White Mountains today were created 124 to 100 million years ago as the North American Plate moved westward over the New England hotspot. Certainly worth a historical visit is the New England Ski Museum.

For those of you looking for a more leisurely and nostalgic view of the mountains you can take the Valley Train departing from Conway and Bartlett. Or join the Notch Train which carries passengers through the spectacular scenery of Crawford Notch in a real life steam engine.

## Photographers (People & Places)

Waterfalls are plentiful in the White Mountains region, due to the winter melt. These were some of my favourites: Bridal Veil Falls, Dixville Notch Cascade and Flume, Flume Gorge, Rocky Gorge, Thomson's Falls and Emerald Pool.

There are also many scenic drives everywhere in the White Mountains, but I would recommend the White Mountains Trail which has been federally designated. Encompassing natural beauty, cultural abundance, historical charm along its 100 mile route.

For more information contact the New Hampshire Division of Travel and Tourism Development or go here: www.visitnh.gov.

Old Man In The Mountain

## Only in America ...
The White Mountains include the Old Man of the Mountain which is New Hampshire's State symbol. Its a rock formation on Cannon Mountain that, when viewed from a certain angle, resembled the distinct craggy profile of a man's face. That was, until bits fell off in May of 2003. Awkward!

Mount Washington, which at 6,288 feet, is the highest mountain in the north eastern U.S. The site used to measure some of the fastest wind gust ever recorded at 231 miles per hour in 1934.

Ever wondered where maple syrup comes from? Join the Sugar Maple program, visitors can see how syrup is made, its history and basic tree identification techniques. wwwtherocks.org.

# USA VOTED - TOP 6 'OTHER' LETTER "W" DESTINATIONS ...

**Williamsburg, Virginia**
Richmond International Airport to Eugene is 52 miles or approx. 1hr 11mins.

**West Chester, Pennsylvania, NY**
Distance to Philadelphia International Airport is 26 miles or approx. 43mins.

**West Palm Beach, Florida**
Distance to Palm Beach International Airport is 5 miles or 11mins.

**Wichita, Kansas**
Distance to Kansas City International Airport is 222 miles or 3hrs 44mins.

**Wausau, Wisconsin**
Richmond International Airport to Eugene is 16 miles or 24mins.

**Walla Walla, Washington**
Distance to Tri-Cities Airport is 60 miles or 1hr 22mins.

# $X$ *is for......* # $X$enia

**Xenia, Illinois -** Blink and You'll Miss It! Xenia consisted of a bank, post office, a tiny government office and a restaurant. The arrival of my now covered memorabilia-clad "Reggie the RV" immediately became The Talk of the Town.

"X" for Xenia, Illinois. I have to admit that not many American's could think of many "X" locations. They may have thought of an "X" letter, but no-one had any idea what state it might be in.

I used to have long debates with people about whether Xanadu was actually a place or not, it is by the way, its in Florida. As it turns out there are 3 Xenia's across the United States the others are in Ohio and Kansas.

It seemed to take a lifetime to get to Xenia in Illinois, I don't think it helped that I was traveling just after the winter snows. So it was damp, wet and miserable. I also seemed to have some level of bad luck in states that began with "I". For example, despite having travelled 45(+) states at this point, it was in Indiana I suffered my first theft which was my fishing rods. Then when I got to Illinois, somebody stole all my wash room toiletries. But undeterred I made my way through Illinois to Xenia.

So here I was in Xenia, Illinois - "Blink and you'll miss It!" It consisted of a bank, a post office, a tiny government office and a restaurant. The arrival of my now covered memorabilia-clad "Reggie the RV" immediately became The Talk of the Town with everyone staring at me.

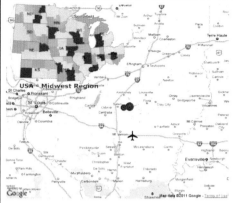

So I went for a small walk around the town, I soon realized I had probably stumbled upon the smallest destination on my tour of America to date.

I later found out that this was in fact true. The population of Xenia according to the 2000 census was only 407 people consisting of 180 households, 96% of which are white.

Having travelled for hundreds of miles, I went into a restaurant for some lunch. On hearing my accent it wasn't long before the questions started: "Where is your accent from? Is that your RV out there?"

# Xenia, Illinois

Before I knew it the whole restaurant knew my business. Then a lady who had just finished her lunch went back to work at the bank next door. It wasn't long before the bank staff arrived to ask the same questions.

It then turned-out that everyone in the bank had contacted people at home, who where coming to meet me. Then the police arrived to check out my RV, then the Mayor had found out. Before I knew it, I was meeting the locally elected representatives in their little office.

I got a nice signed menu from the restaurant owner, a book about Xenia from the Mayor.

And a mug from the lady from the bank with Xenia on it. This was the second mug I got. The first mug I was given had been a gift from someone and was her favourite so it had to be switched out!

Lots of photographs later with what felt like everyone from the town. As fast as I had arrived, I was gone.

Thank you to everyone at Xenia for making me feel so welcome, I will never forget you. Who knows maybe I will be able to return the favour one day.

Next stop Wyoming....

# USA VOTED - TOP 6 'OTHER' LETTER "X" DESTINATIONS ...

**Xanadu, Florida**
To NW Florida Beaches International Airport to Eugene is 28 miles or 45mins.

**Xavier, Ohio**
Distance to Cincinnati Northern Kentucky International Airport is 30 miles or 25mins.

**Xenophon, Tennessee**
Distance to Palm Beach International Airport is 236 miles or 4hrs 7mins.

**X-Crossing, Montana**
Distance to Billings Logan International Airport is 258 miles or 5hrs 34mins.

**X-Prairie, Mississippi**
To Phillips International Airport to Eugene is 45 miles or 1hr 5mins.

**X Rollercoaster, 6 Flags, California**
Distance to Van Nuys Airport is 21 miles or approx. 35mins.

# $Y$ *is for......*   $Y$ ellowstone

**Yellowstone, Wyoming -** Although now a major tourist destination, you get a glimpse into what America was like, before Americans. Yellowstone will be a truly personal experience. One you'll never forget.

"Y" is for Yellowstone National Park, Wyoming/Montana. Both Yellowstone and Yosemite, California had been neck and neck throughout my journey across America. In fact, Yellowstone beat Yosemite by just a handful of Votes in the end.

To be respectful to those Votes, I did visit both National Parks in the end. I found them both to be amazingly beautiful, but also distinctly different. Yellowstone is pre-historic, huge in size and alive with nature. In comparison Yosemite is smaller but equally as beautiful with stunning mountains, waterfalls, lakes and lush valleys. But Yellowstone is truly unique place because of its volcanic and thermal landscape.

To get to Yellowstone most people go through Wyoming, by accident I came across Devils Tower. If you see a sign for it, pull in, for no other reason than for its comedic value. Anyone familiar with the film Close Encounters of the Third Kind and the Richard Dreyfuss Mashed Potato scene will recognize it instantly. The top-hat shaped 2,000ft high rock looks like it belongs on the moon rather than in the middle of no-where in Wyoming.

I had been to Yellowstone on two occasions, the first time due to the weather when I tried to get to the park entrance there were signs saying "Closed"! So I would advise you to make a thorough assessment of the time of year and weather before setting off. Having now travelled 48 States and 25 letters, it was going to take a lot more snow to stop me now!

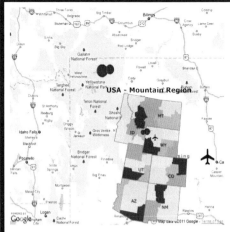

Eventually I did see the park in the winter with a guide and a snowmobile. Luckily for me the nature of my journey meant I could be very flexible. But many people are caught out by Yellowstone's very long and isolating winters.

So before setting off, I would advise planning your journey. Just like the Grand Canyon getting to Yellowstone can be challenging because there are so many entrances and GPS systems aren't that reliable.

Pop on Google maps directions - Cody, Wyoming to Yellowstone, Wyoming and you'll see what I mean. Its bizarre one of the biggest visitor sites in the US and getting there is like the Bermuda Triangle.

# Yellowstone National Park, Wyoming

Also because of the weather and height of some of the elevations physically travelling there can be alittle hairy. Especially in an RV!

The first time around I went via Cody and the Wyoming side, which is generally quite flat. If you get a chance stop off at the Buffalo Bill Museum, I would highly recommend it.

Surprisingly large it has a huge armory display, a Buffalo Bill archive and a fantastic little art gallery featuring works from the pioneering days to present. The works of art showing off the region beautifully.

If the National Park itself is outside your price range then Cody is a good place to stay and drive into Yellowstone daily. There is a good selection of restaurants and hotels throughout Cody to meet everyone's price range.

If you arrive via the Montana entrance, again you may find your GPS lets you down so make sure you have a map to hand.

You are likely to go through Red Lodge which is also worth a stop off for lunch, souvenir shopping and a walk around.

You are also likely to go through The Bear Tooth Ranger District and Custer National Forest covering 1.3million acres. With elevations ranging from 1,000 to 12,000ft this bendy, steep road is not for the nervous driver.

Whichever route you venture on, take your time and don't rush it. You will be rewarded with views of snow capped mountains, deep valleys and huge lakes.

Also worth some pre-planning are the organized tours like horse back riding, snow mobiling, fishing and hunting. If you haven't booked well in advance you will be disappointed. I also found a similar story with much of the hotel accommodation.

There are a range of accommodation types at Yellowstone, but I personally would recommend camping. Although the facilities are limited (no electric) it seems a shame to be cooped-up in a hotel when you are surrounded by Yellowstone.

CAUTION
DO NOT APPROACH
WILDLIFE

Camping with a wood fire seems to make it all the more natural.

Bears though are a genuine concern, at each camping spot you are given a bear-proof cabinet to put all your food in. A Ranger told me "if you are grilling food, make sure you stay watching it. Leaving it, even for a minute, will tempt the wildlife to come and grab it".

I thought this was a bit over-the-top until a herd of buffalo came through the camp the next morning and trashed it! "Yes Sir, Mr Ranger, Sir!"

# Yellowstone National Park, Wyoming

If you can, avoid Yellowstone in the height of the summer when US children are off on vacation. Normally mid-June to the start of September the place will be incredibly crowded. Yellowstone received 3.2 million visitors in 2007, the record for a year. The other thing to note is that it has a very small hotel ratio with only around 9 and only 7 campsites.

So if you are able to I would advise going late spring or early fall just as the park is opening or closing for the winter. It still receives around 100,000 visitors at that time of year, so it is not exactly quiet, but a noticeable different.

If you are a wildlife fanatic then a winter visit is a must. Because the vast array of wildlife (67 types of mammals alone) make their way down to the lower valley's to feed and escape the blistering cold at the higher elevations. Plus there is virtually no-one around to scare them off.

I was lucky enough to see a Beaver, a Wolf, Long Horn Ram, an Elk Bull and my favourite a Mountain Ram. These were really cute, a pure white ball of fur with tiny horns.

To fully appreciate Yellowstone it is important to know some of the key facts before you visit:

Yellowstone is the world's first National Park designated by President Grant and Congress in 1872 and spans an area of 3,472 square miles.

The equivalent of 2.2 billion acres. It is larger than Rhode Island and Delaware combined.

End-to-end it would be the distance between San Francisco to Boston.

Yellowstone Lake is one of the largest high-altitude lakes in North America.

The lake is centred over the Yellowstone Caldera, the largest Super Volcano in the world. The park experiences approximately 1,000–3,000 earthquakes annually.

Half of the world's geothermal features are in Yellowstone. It has approximately 10,000 thermal features and more than 300 geysers. Steamboat Geyser is the largest geyser in the world still erupting.

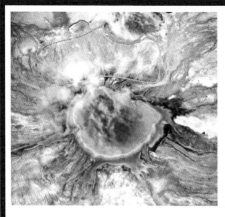

The Caldera Super Volcano, considered an active volcano measures approximately 45 by 30 miles. The crater top alone is some 1,500 square miles. The equivalent of a 4 State journey from Los Angeles to Kansas City.

It has erupted with tremendous force several times in the last two million years. To put this into context, the 1980 Mount St. Helens eruption blew 1,300 vertical feet off the mountain.

It ejected a column 80,000 feet high in 15 minutes and 1.4 billion cubic yards of ash detectable over 22,000 square miles away. Killing 57 people.

# Yellowstone National Park, Wyoming

The last major eruption at Yellowstone, some 640,000 years ago, ejected 8,000 times the ash and lava of Mount St. Helens.

These facts are important because most people who visit Yellowstone, don't fully appreciate that if "it ever blows" it would be Game Over! The Discovery Channel estimated it would take out most of North America, killing millions and have a massive impact on the ecological system of the world. They predict it could happen one day, but do not know when. Yikes!

For people who have never experienced geothermal sights before Yellowstone is truly a unique sight, especially in the USA. But for the people who are worldly travelled and have seen geothermal sights before it will not be so impressive.

Here I am thinking of the North Island in New Zealand or Iceland. But Yellowstone is a truly unique place and certainly a 'bucket list' destination.

I was lucky enough to see it two ways, once was in the dead of winter and once in the height of summer. In the dead of winter the park was "officially" closed but after some serious pestering I managed to persuade a guide who owned some snow mobiles to show me around. This I have to say was truly magical and I felt very privileged as there was virtually no-one around.

In the winter the first thing that strikes you is the stillness of the place. But at an elevation of over 7,500ft it was freezing !

The best bit though is the accessibility of the wildlife. Abandoning the higher baron cold landscape, you find them in the lower valleys looking to feed. I saw more wildlife in 1 hour in the winter than I saw throughout my entire summer visit.

Seeing my first American Bison in the wild was a thrill, as they have virtually been wiped out across most of America. In case you get into a debate about it, Buffalo and Bison are completely different animals. Bison are very shaggy with a hump, the confusion has arisen because the native bison has usually been *called* buffalo.

In America you are only likely to see Buffalo on the menu in Montana or Wyoming (Bison are protected). So make sure you take advantage of it if you can. For me it had the texture of fillet of beef but with a gamey taste. My first bison/buffalo burger, delicious.

*Y* *is for......*    Y ellowstone

Unlike the summer, the attractions in the winter seem to just appear above the layers and layers of snow. The main difference is that you see everything from a snow mobile instead of by foot.

You also have to be alittle more careful in case you drive straight off a ravine because there are no trail signs or roads!

If you are lucky enough to visit Yellowstone, this map shows you the main attractions.

If you take a trip, these are normally the main stops :

1. Old Faithful Geyser and Upper Geyser Basin

2. Grand Canyon of the Yellowstone

3. Hayden Valley

4. Mammoth Hot Springs

5. Yellowstone Lake

6. Norris Geyser Basin

7. Lamar Valley

8. Tower Fall

9. Lower Geyser Basin / Fountain Paint Pots

10. West Thumb Geyser Basin

You can do your own research, so here I will just give you the basics and need to knows.

Old Faithfull

Set around a huge visitors centers with gift shops, coffee stands and a full buffet restaurant.

Old Faithfull is in fact only 1 of numerous other geysers within walking distance that erupt. You will find the eruption times posted somewhere around the visitor center.

So if Geysers are your thing, then you could spend half a day walking around the Upper Basin. As it boasts the largest concentration of geysers in the world.

Many of them are in fact more impressive than Old Faithful itself. Including many of the worlds largest geysers called Castle, Daisy, Grand and Riverside. After Old Faithfull I would definitely check out Grand Geyser which roughly erupts every 9 hours.

In the summer it goes without saying, arrive at least 30 minutes before predicted eruption in order to get a good spot.

Just like if you want to eat at the restaurant (note: you can't see Old Faithfull from it) it may be worth booking in advance.

### Grand Canyon of Yellowstone

This for me, was the best view at Yellowstone and seems to be the picture everyone has. In the winter the landscape was still apart from this forceful waterfall. In the summer it is great to just sit and watch it, funny people watching as well. Try to sit out of the way, so you don't end up being the "Say Cheese" photographer for everyone.

### Hayden Valley

This seems to be where the wildlife like to graze, so there are normally lots of people around.

# Yellowstone National Park, Wyoming

Having just dumped their cars, there is a lot of general hubbub. Admittedly it is a nice view of the valley below and certainly a good picture, but the wildlife are too far away to see without a telescopic lens. But your curiosity will get the better of you, so go and take in the hysteria.

### Mammoth Hot Springs

This is a large geothermal site covered in hot springs. The colours of an artists pallet, bubbling down a hill of limestone and minerals. Near the edge of the park on the Montana border, it is a popular place for people to stay.

### Yellowstone Lake

As it is close to all the major camp sites like Fishing and Bay Bridge, you cannot really miss Yellowstone Lake. Yellowstone Lake has 136 square miles of surface area and 110 miles of shoreline. It is the largest lake at high elevation in North America (above 7,000 ft.). With its deepest spot in excess of 390 ft.

It is a natural lake and has fish in it, but fishing is prohibited. Mainly due to problems of over population of non native species. Power boating is at a limited speed and the temperature only just makes it above zero in the height of summer, so don't go jumping in!

### Norris Geyser Basin

Another geothermal spot it is home to a number of bubbling hot pools and geysers including the largest active geyser in the world Steamboat Geyser.

It is considered to be one of the most active parts of the park being closer to the magma than any of the other basins.

### Norris Geyser Basin

Steamboat's eruptions can last anywhere from 3 to 40 minutes in length with water being thrown more than 300 feet (90m) into the air.

The problem is not many people have seen it because Steamboat is not predictable. With recorded intervals between major eruptions being anywhere from 4 days to 50 years. Once the geyser was dormant from 1911 to 1961.

I have seen clips of it on You Tube and it looks and sounds awesome. Who knows, you could be one the few people in the world to actually see it.

# Yellowstone National Park, Wyoming

### Lamar Valley

This is Yellowstone in a snapshot, a lush green valley, a trout filled stream and buffalo grazing in the distance. If you want to do some fly fishing then this is consider one of the best places. Remember though, Where there's Fish, There's Bears!

### Tower Fall

Tower Creek's confluence with the Yellowstone River drops 132 ft (40m) and is accessible at the top or down a small trail into the canyon. If the trail is open (often its washed away) make the effort to go down and see it at the bottom.

### Lower Geyser Basin / Fountain Paint Pots

This is the most popular of the geothermal areas because it is the largest and the thermal features are clumped close together.

Here you will see bubbling mud pools (formed by escaping sulphide and carbon dioxide), geysers, springs, and fumaroles. They have names like Silex Spring, Fountain Paint Pots, Clepsydra Geyser (Clepsydra is Greek for water clock). Then sounding like a thousand kettles boiling the Red Spouter. The temperature of them is around 200 degrees Fahrenheit.

This is a truly unique sight, there are colours you will see that I don't think even have a name in the English language. On the way there look out for rising steam on the horizon.

### West Thumb Geyser Basin

West Thumb Geyser Basin is one of the smallest geyser basins in Yellowstone yet its location along the shore of Yellowstone Lake ranks as the most scenic.

No geysers, instead you have the multi-coloured springs, pools, mud pots, fumaroles and lake shore geysers. Right on the side of Yellowstone Lake it is a poplar spot for kayaking.

Fishing Cone along the lake shore is a symmetrical cone just underneath the waterline. It has been popularized by early stories of people cooking trout in the boiling hot cone.

So that concludes all the major sights of Yellowstone. Whether you go in the winter or summer to Yellowstone, one thing I can guarantee is it is a truly unique experience.

# Yellowstone National Park, Wyoming

In the winter, you can miss many of the landmarks because of the layers and layers of snow. It wasn't until I went back in the summer that I realized I had almost completely missed the 136 mile wide Yellowstone Lake the first time around. Because it was frozen and completely covered in snow!

Seeing Yellowstone in its most dormant state and in almost isolation was unique. I sat and watched Old Faithfull erupt completely alone. I didn't appreciate it until I went back in the summer and I was surrounded by hundreds and hundreds of people.

But this experience would not be for everyone, there are no gift shops, no toilets, just you and hundreds of bears! At night it was alittle scary.

Suffering from PTSD I had lost the ability to feel any fear. Hell, I had faced all my worst fears only a few years before. So freezing temperatures and a few bears weren't going to scare me off!

Yellowstone is nature at its most pure, I applaud President Ulysses S. Grant for having the foresight to make at least one small part of America sacred.

Each person will like it for different reasons. It could be the mud pools, the scenery, the wildlife, the waterfalls, the geysers.

One night I woke up in the middle of the night and on venturing outside my tent I looked-up at the night sky. It literally took my breath away, the canopy of stars were like a giant sparkling dot-to-dot. The pristine nature of the park and the elevations making this sight possible.

I was so taken with it, I re-lit the fire and sat staring up at it until morning.

For me, Yellowstone in the winter had provided a much needed sense of calm. It was the first time in along time I had felt peace and free of the demons in my mind. Whilst here, I think it was the first time in nearly 2 years that I hadn't had a nightmare.

Corny, I know, but it gave me an appreciation of how insignificant we all are on a scale of things. It had made me start to appreciate my A to Zee journey a little more.

I knew I was certainly lucky to have done it. To have had the time, the money and the sheer guts to do this journey in the first place.

Yellowstone underlined this for me, it isn't the touristy things. But the sense of isolation, and being submerged in this untamed wilderness. It truly is a "personal experience" one that will be different for everyone.

One, that you will never forget.

# IF YOU HAVE MORE TIME ...

## Outdoors People

There are numerous winter pursuits to enjoy at Yellowstone like snow-shoeing, ski-ing & boarding and snow-mobiling. The greater Yellowstone region is fast becoming a dog-sledding destination for both recreational and serious racing. Many companies—especially in north-western Wyoming between Dubois and Jackson—offer dog-sled tours. In late January-February you can see the largest sled dog race in the lower 48 states; the International Pedigree Stage Stop Sled Dog Race. This thrilling race traverses almost 450 miles of Wyoming backcountry.

In the summer you can enjoy climbing, hiking, fishing, water rafting, horse back riding and biking. It us unusual for a National Park to allow you to do such activities, so take advantage of them. You could honestly stay at Yellowstone for weeks if you wanted as there is plenty to do. But winter or summer make sure you book well in advance for any activities.

## History, Culture & Gifts

The history of Yellowstone's people dates back around 11,000 years when it was inhabited by native Americans. The first Europeans arrived at the park around 200 years ago and in 1872 it became the worlds first National Park. Today there are around 1,600 archaeological sites to enjoy and 67 different species of mammals.

Yellowstone is home to about half of the world's geysers—the largest concentration on earth. Including the famous Old Faithful which currently erupts around 20 times a day. It can be predicted with a 90% confidence rate within a 10 minute variation. Check for posted prediction times at the Old Faithful Visitors Centre.

## Photographers (People & Places)

It is difficult to photograph Yellowstone because of its size and scale. For example, there are around 10,000 thermal features, 300 geysers and 290 waterfalls. With more than 24 sites including landmarks and districts being on the National Register of Historic Places. My advice would be to just buy a book about it and enjoy the experience.

The Park is quite easy to navigate as there are scenic spots around every corner, the more popular ones tend to have a range of facilities like restaurants and gift shops. My advise would be to take some kind of tour as they will take you to all the best spots in one day. You can always circle back to them at your leisure later.

## Only in America.....

In the mid-1800s, prospectors scoured the streams of the greater Yellowstone area looking for gold. Throughout the region, historic gold-mining districts still hold annual festivals. In Wyoming, gold prospectors can be found hard at work panning for gold in the South Pass Area near Lander. Montana's many coloured sapphires, mined here since 1892, are found in the famous Placer Gravels near Philipsburg. You can mine your own in the summer at Gem Mountain, and year round at the Sapphire Gallery.

If there is a mass of people all crowding around one spot in Yellowstone, this will be because there will some kind of wildlife close-by. Normally impossible to see, so don't crash or dump your car and get a ticket. It will probably be an anti-climax and not worth the ticket. Sorry !

# USA VOTED - TOP 6 'OTHER' LETTER "Y" DESTINATIONS ...

### Yosemite National Park, California
Distance to Sacramento International Airport is 183 miles or approx. 3hrs 35mins.

### Yale, Connecticut
Distance to Bradley International Airport is 52 miles or 1 hour.

### Yonkers, New York City
Distance to LaGuardia Airport is 15 miles or approx. 23mins.

### Yorktown, Virginia
Distance to Newport-News Williamsburg International Airport is 12 miles or approx. 24mins.

### Yuma, AZ
Distance to Palm Springs International Airport is 169 miles or approx. 3hrs 5mins.

### Yucca Valley, California
Distance to Palm Springs International Airport is 38 miles or 10mins.

# Z is for...... Zion

**Zion National Park, Utah** - The State of Utah has 'screen-saver' scenery around every corner with Zion National Park as it's crowning glory. America had saved the best 'till last and the perfect ending to my A to Zee journey.

"Zee" is for the Zion National Park, Utah. It was tinged with happiness and some relief that I was on my way through Utah to my final destination. Here I was, 50 States and Provinces later, 80,000 (+) miles and slightly saner than I was when I set-off.

Strangely though it was the silly things which I was reminiscing about now like; "How many times did I try Fried Green tomatoes, before deciding I didn't like them? Or "How many forms of transport have I been in?" Or "How many different types of foods have I tried?"

I think the biggest question of all was "Did I feel any better?" The reason I had set off on this journey in the first place was to try to reduce my PTSD symptoms. I had certainly looped all the way across America, had my daily horrific nightmares and panic attacks. But I was feeling as though maybe I had left some of my demons somewhere along the way.

In one sense PTSD had been a constant companion with symptoms like hyper-vigilance, no fear and lack of emotions keeping me safe. As for what I had left behind a good job, beachside apartment, nice car (etc) all those things had paled into insignificance.

The one thing that had got me through this journey had been the memory of Ozzy John, my late husband. I felt like he had taken every step with me, enjoyed every sunset and been watching over me during this incredibly difficult time in my life.

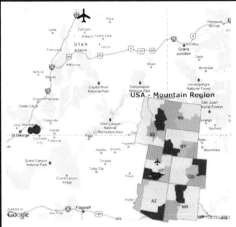

Thankfully America had saved the best till last, the fantastic State of Utah. So taken by it, I decided to rename it the Screensaver State. Because if you take any standard PC screen-saver, I can guarantee you most of the shots will be of Utah.

To see what I mean log into Google Images and type-in just these 4 and you will immediately understand :

1) Delicate Arch, UT
2) Rainbow Bridge, UT
3) Monument Valley, UT
4) Dead Horse Point, UT.

# Zion National Park, Utah

These 4 only scratch the surface and there are hundreds of places to visit all across Utah. But because many of the visitor attractions in Utah are not as well-known as places like Yellowstone, The Grand Canyon and Niagara Falls you can still see them in relative isolation.

An example of this was when I went to Dead Horse Point State Park. From the camp ground I decided to walk to one of the visitor spots.

Off the beaten track, I made my way through a clearing to a sight I will never forget. A huge gorge, equal the Grand Canyon and views to rival it.

The layered rock formations all the colours of the rainbow flowing into the canyon below. I was completely alone sat on a cliff edge, looking down into the deep canyon.

I was so taken by it, I sat there for a good hour just listening to the wind and taking in the tremendous view as the sun began to set. I thought to myself "I Love Utah".

Everywhere I went it was like that. I have counted at least 128 official visitor attractions, but there must be hundreds and hundreds. Most make up the Grand Circle tour which would be my recommended way to see them.

So having come from Yellowstone into Utah and not really knowing where to start I decided I would head to the capital of Utah, Salt Lake City. As it is centrally located and to the north, it meant I could do a huge circular loop and see as much of the State as possible.

## Salt Lake City

Looks like most other US Cities, but not as sprawling and with lots more Mormons (aka) Latter Day Saints making up the population.

It is known for skiing and its Salt Lake which is the second saltiness body of water in the world. But be warned, to see any semblance of it you have to go in the height of summer and the shallow ponds at Stansbury Island.

But the biggest pull in Utah are winter sports. Snow starts falling in November through March. Famed as having "The Greatest Snow on Earth" which appears on many of Utah's licence plates. Skiing alone is a 500 million dollar annual industry in Utah.

With Salt Lake's 12,000 ft Wasatch Mountains offering some of Utah's highest most picturesque and rugged peaks.

# Z is for...... Zion

I cannot talk about Utah and Salt Lake City without mentioning the Mormons. For those of you who know nothing about theology here is my version of "The Dummies Guide to Mormons!"

An east coast native called Joseph Smith was the founder of the Mormons around 1820. Today a vast majority of Mormons are members of The Church of Jesus Christ of Latter-day Saints.

They are famous in Utah because in 1847, the first party of Mormon emigrants led by Brigham Young reached the Salt Lake Valley which eventually became the Utah Territory.

They believe in dedicating large amounts of time and resources (3 hour services on a Sunday) to their church.

They tend to be very family-oriented, and have strong connections across generations and extended family.

A common misconception is that Mormons have hundreds of wives. Polygamy was a distinguishing practice of many early Mormons; however it was renounced by The LDS Church in 1890 and discontinued with a handful of high profile cases and Acts of Congress.

Today the practice is illegal in all 50 States and only practiced by breakaway so-called Mormon Fundamentalist in secret .

Mormons also have a strict law of chastity (thoughts and actions) requiring abstention from sexual relations outside of marriage.

You also tend to find that Mormons believe in strict fidelity so don't cheat on each other. Divorce is highly frowned upon.

They have a strict health code that prohibits alcoholic beverages, tobacco, coffee, tea and other addictive substances. Yawn!

They use the Bible and Book of Mormon and believe the authority to perform such ordinance was restored through Joseph Smith. That their church is guided by living prophets and apostles.

They have a unique view of cosmology, and believe that all people are spirit-children of God.

They believe that returning to God requires following the example of Jesus Christ, accepting his atonement through specific ordinances such as baptism. Central to Mormon faith is the belief that God speaks to his children and answers their prayers.

Mormons' history has shaped them into a people with a strong sense of unity and community. From their early beginnings Mormons have tried to establish what they call Zion, a utopian society of the righteous. Smith had tried to literally build a city called Zion, to which converts gathered.

The reason all this is important is because around 68% of the population of Utah are Mormom. But interestingly they are not that easy to spot, unlike the Amish that dress differently and tend to live off the land.

Mormons seem to blend into the community a lot more and can be quite secretive.

Here are my top tips to turn your "Mo-Dar" on:

- They tend to wear excessive underclothing garments on a boiling hot day called the Celestial Smile. To avoid "temptation from evil".

- If you ask them about their family if they describe 11 sisters, 19 brothers and 69 cousins that's normally a dead give-away.

- If you get some very strong views on gay marriage; firstly remember you are in fanatically religious America! But Mormons generally only support a traditional (heterosexual) marriage union.

# Zion National Park , Utah

My experience with Mormons was that if you were genuinely interested in what they believe, they were cool talking about it. I have to admit to having a secret chuckle at some of their more fundamental views on life.

There is one thing for sure, I couldn't be a Mormon, not even for a day! I would commit too many sins! But Each to their Own, I Say.

Having left the Mormons in Salt Lake City I was now heading south towards the Unita Mountains. These are great to visit if you are prepared to put in the effort, as there are a dozen peaks rising above 13,000ft. So come prepared, have a map or hand-held GPS. No park Rangers here if you get stuck. It will be worth it though, I enjoyed blue skies, lush green meadows, brightly coloured wild flowers and clear sparkling streams.

Heading northeast there is the point where the four major rivers of Utah (Duchesne, Provo, Bear and Weber) meet and is the perfect spot for camping and fishing. Here I was lucky enough to see lots and lots of dear in the wild. Beautifully shy the slightest movement made them scarper. As soon as you got your shotgun out (joking!) Your camera out; whoosh, they where gone.

Travelling further north and east of Utah is River Country and attracts all kinds of river enthusiasts. It was in the Green River, Arizona I had first tried water rafting. Little did I know at the time, it actually starts its life up in Utah.

You can look 2,000ft down into the Green River and Whirlpool Canyon at Harper's Corner Trail with its whirlpools of swirling currents. So perfect for canoe or kayak enthusiasts.

I would also recommend a visit to the red and orange sandstone walls of Split Mountain and Flaming Gorge. Here the Green River emerges from miles of rugged canyons with 12 types of dinosaur having been found here at Morrison Formation since 1909.

Heading even further south now I would checkout the San Rafael Swell, Castle Country region and Slot Canyon. Which is full of weird and wonderfully shaped rock formations to try and squeeze through. Again come prepared to hike and then spend the night sleeping under the stars.

My next recommendation in this area would be Lake Powell. For me it was magical, this was my Disneyland.

I loved everything about it, the sunrise, the heat during the day, the boating activities and Wi-fi (which is quite important when you are researching a book!) Open fire, no people around, good facilities. Then the sunsets...oh, the sunsets, nothing like them. One evening the whole lake turned Barbie Pink. I could not believe my eyes!

Even better, you can use Lake Powell as your base to pop off and see something new everyday. I would start at Vermillion Cliffs, another popular screen saver shot.

# Zion National Park, Utah

I had spent some time in Vermillion, Ohio and had an amazing welcome. So I had to go and check it out and Facebook all my Vermillion friends back in Ohio. Stepping into these swirling caves of browns, gold and reds is like being in the middle of a Belgium chocolate.

For a similar unique scene check out Coral Pink Sand Dunes, the pink sands are formed by erosion of the surrounding cliffs. Then see Calf Creek Falls in the Grand Staircase-Escalante National Monument. For any amateur photographers this will be your screen saver journey now complete.

At this point you can get a bit weary of all the fantastic sights you have seen. So I recommend, stopping and camping and getting alittle isolation to digest before moving on. There is *so* much to see in Utah it can get a bit overwhelming.

Next stop before Zion will normally be Bryce Canyon, another "must-see". It is a series of rock formations looking like surface coral extending down 1,000 ft through pink and white limestone in the Paunsaugunt Plateau. It is like looking at the Great Barrier Reef without the sea. This whole area is great for accommodation, as Zion is normally busy.

So after that amazing tour of Utah, I have finally arrived at my final destination the entry gate at Zion National Park. I am so excited I run around like a schoolgirl asking strangers for photographs with anything that has the words Zion on it.

I grab every Park Ranger and have my photo with them until I am politely asked to move along!

I can hardly believe it I have finally made it; 3 years in the making, over 80,000 miles, 26 destinations, 50 states and provinces and thousands of Votes. Hooray!

I am so excited I miss all the important instructions regarding driving through the park itself. Driving, because normally in peak season you are ushered onto trams that take you through the park with rangers.

So here we are again me and Reggie the RV on some the narrowest roads and deepest drops in America. Arrgh!

Regardless I ventured into the park remembering the RV sticker I was given as a gift in Texas that said "Warning: Driver Brakes Hard For Scenery!"

Mount Carmel highway winds its way through Zion providing breath taking views of its deep canyons and multi coloured rocks. All with appropriately grandiose names like Temple, Patriarch, Thrones and Cathedrals.

Long ago their mere presence fomented fear in the Paiute Indians who refused to stay here after dark. I could see why, it does feel quite supernatural once inside its deep shadowy canyons.

# Zion National Park, Utah

The most famous of them being The White Throne or Angels Landing, this long windy trail drops you into Zion's heart. Aptly name by Frederick V. Fisher a Methodist minister, it certainly lives up to its divine name.

Walking down it, I was reminded of my journey down into the Grand Canyon from the top rim down to the Colorado River below.

Like then, take your time and stop often. Submerge yourself around 3,000 feet of sheer rock face and the explosion on the senses.

One thing to note is that there are 2 types of visitors to Angels Landing. There is the "Just Fancy a Gentle Hike" people. Then there are the "Daredevil Visitors". Get these 2 mixed-up at your peril!

Because the latter involves climbing (and I mean climbing) up some very steep rock faces with little else between you and certain death than steel chains to drag yourself up the steep rock faces. America is normally health and safety crazy, so it was good to get so up-close and personal to Zion.

Try to make sure you give yourself at least a day or even a stop-over if you can and camp. You will reach elevations around 1,500-2000ft and the hikes are a minimum of around 4 miles heading towards Emerald Canyon.

Please note though this hike requires permits, reservations and pre-planning with the Ranger services. So they know who to inform if you fall off the side, I guess!

I think this was the highlight of my trip to Zion. Pardon the pun, but Angels Landing for its fantastic views, lush emerald canyon and towering rocks was simply heavenly.

You will have seen almost half the national park by now, so make your way back onto the main road. Driving through, look out for the phenomenon called Weeping Rock. Were water from above filters to the outside of the rock face, making it seem as though the rock is oozing out water or "weeping".

Eventually you will hit Iron Mountain and the Carmel Tunnel. Completed in 1930, more than a mile long it takes nerves of steel to drive. Due to the size of my RV, oncoming traffic had to be stopped to allow me to drive straight down the middle of it. "Reggie" thought this was awesome!

# Z is for......

# Zion

This was a tad bit scary, trying not to scrape the sides, but once on the other side the view took my breath-away. Wow! America had Saved The Best Till' Last.

From the darkness and claustrophobia of the tunnel, Zion opens out into a huge canyon surrounded by the vivid colours of thousands of years of rock formations. A geologists idea of heaven.

You will be looking at The Switchback, the Great Arch of Zion and the Kolob Arch.

The Kolob is the world's largest arch whose span measures 310 feet or 94 meters. "Reggie the RV" proudly posed in-front of it for his Final Official Picture on the A to Zee journey.

If you can stay longer, research some of the more isolated spots, the effort will be worth it.

I had read about the Emerald Pools and went in search of them. I was rewarded after my hike with three waterfalls at the end of the picturesque trail in the Zion Canyon. Fantastic.

But in reality you can easily see Zion in an afternoon. Whatever route (or rowt, as American's pronounce it) you take, you are likely to find yourself at the Visitors Centre.

There are some great gifts and very knowledgeable people who can tell you everything about the Park and the area.

I loved Zion, it was much better that the Grand Canyon or Yosemite for me. Just one recommendation "See it again and again and again and again..."

So this was it, 3 years in the making I had finally done it. What a journey it had been.

My next stop was to drop "Reggie" off at his new home. Covered in memorabilia from the journey, he had found a permanent home at one of America's largest automobile museums in Tacoma, Washington.

LeMay Marymount were happy to receive Reggie as my charitable donation. Here he could retire and hang out with the other cool cars! Bet none of them have travelled all 50 States!

It was nice to leave some positive semblance of me somewhere in America. Rather than the dramatic stories of John's death, my lock-up, feelings of betrayal and negative press around legal cases.

I'll miss America and the people that I met. One thing I had proven to myself, was that no matter how dark my torturous battled with mental health issues had been.

If I simply kept going, regardless of the path. One day I would get somewhere.

Even if it wasn't where I thought it would be when I took the first step....

# IF YOU HAVE MORE TIME ...

## Outdoors People

Skiing in Utah is a big deal and there are hundreds of famous destinations to research. Personally I would go east of Ogden to Snow Basin. Considered the best kept "powder secret" in Utah with over 400 inches of snow fall annually.

If you prefer water sports head north to the Utah/Idaho border towards Garden City and go to Bear Lake. Here you can enjoy all kinds of water activities including sailing, water-skiing and speed boating. There is a sailing regatta held regularly in the summer. Alternatively, south of Salt Lake City is Utah Lake. The largest natural body of fresh water in the State and is extremely popular for fishing, pleasure boating or water-skiing with the backdrop of the Wasatch Mountains.

If you like caving then you will probably like the limestone formations found in Timpanogos Cave. There are actually three caves connected by man-made tunnels, inside are hundreds of beautifully coloured stalactites and stalagmites.

## History, Culture & Gifts

People have occupied the landscape of the Zion National Park for thousands of years. Zion's first residents tracked mammoths, camels and other mammals through open desert and sheltered canyons. Over the next 1,500 years, a community of farmers known as Ancestral Puebloans evolved. The diverse geological setting gave them a combination rare in deserts: terraces to grow food, a river for water and an adequate growing season. But drought, resource depletion and migrations eventually decreased the Ancestral Puebloans dominance. Westward expansion eventually brought early Mormon pioneers to the canyon in 1860s, who built small communities and farmed the river terraces.

Since then Utah is famous for its Mormon heritage, they built Logan Temple in 1877 of hard siliceous limestone from Logan Canyon. Officially you cannot enter, so you may want to have a sentence like this up your sleeve "Can I see the progressive room for presentation of the endowment, I believe it is lovely!"

## Photographers (People & Places)

You are spoilt for choice in Utah, so as well as the usual visitor spots try these:

Cecret Lake in Little Cottonwood Canyon is a 1 mile long reaching an elevation of 9,800ft with fantastic views.

Great Salt Lake State Park is Utah's second largest state park containing 23,000 acres of land where bison and antelope roam at Antelope Island.

Head to Logan in the northern tip of Utah. Take in the panoramic views of Logan Canyon. It extends about 30 miles from its mouth to a summit pass on the Bear River range with some fantastic views year-round.

## Only in America.....

Balanced Rock standing 55 ft tall defies nature as it precariously sits atop a pedestal 73ft tall with the snow covered La Sal Mountains as the backdrop. This can be an amusing photograph for you and your mates trying to push it off!

I would also check out Delicate Arch near Moab so named because it is the most delicate of the Arches National Park, so see it before it collapses.

Interested in Mormon culture then you should head to Main and Temple Street in Salt lake City here you will find a myriad of Mormon monuments, tabernacles and everything Mormon. You can also join a Pioneer Trolley which will take you through all the Mormon sites in the area.

# USA VOTED - TOP 6 'OTHER' LETTER "Z" DESTINATIONS ...

**Zephyr Cove, Nevada**
Distance to Sacramento International Airport is 124 miles or 2hrs 38mins.

**Zebulon, North Carolina, GA & KY**
Distance to Raleigh-Durham International Airport is 40 miles or 46mins

**Zillah, Washington**
Distance to Bowers Airport is 61 miles or 1hr 7mins.

**Zachery, Louisiana**
Distance to Baton Rouge Municipal Airport is 14 miles or 24mins.

**Zumbrota, MN**
Distance to St Paul International Airport is 60 miles or 1hr 5mins.

**Zuni, New Mexico**
Distance to Gallup Municipal Airport is 42 miles or 52mins.

*T*he *E*nd

Reading this book you may wonder "Why do this journey?"

The motivation for doing this journey is born out of a series of sad and tragic events. The sudden death of her husband and getting diagnosed with a mental illness. Kay was first diagnosed with PTSD in November 2008, six months after John died.

Sadly ignorance to mental health issues resulted in her being wrongfully institutionalized where she was subjected to further trauma. Making her symptoms even worse.

Despite this since April 2009 she has been seeing PTSD Specialists both in the US and UK. Three years on, although recovery remains slow, it is certainly in the right direction.

This book reminds us all that information regarding mental illness is readily available and how important it is to - Get Educated.

------------

This journey is a testament to the fact that:

*"When a Sh\*t Mountain Lands on Top of You.*

*Firstly you Have to Find the Spade.*
*Then Start Shoveling!*

*This Book is Dedicated to the People Who;*
*Despite Everything, Have kept Shoveling*
*with Me.*

*And to You, if you are currently trying to*
*Find the Spade!"*

**Post-traumatic stress disorder (PTSD)** is a type of anxiety disorder. It can occur after you've seen or experienced a traumatic event that involved the threat of injury or death.

Causes, incidence, and risk factors

PTSD can occur at any age. It can follow a natural disaster such as a flood or fire, or events such as: Sudden Death, Rape, Domestic Violence, Prison Stay (etc).

The cause of PTSD is unknown. Psychological, genetic, physical, and social factors are involved.

PTSD changes the body's response to stress. It affects the stress hormones and chemicals that carry information between the nerves (neurotransmitters). It is not known why traumatic events cause PTSD in some people but not others.

Symptoms of PTSD fall into three main categories:

### 1. "Reliving" the event, which disturbs day-to-day activity:

* Flashback episodes, where the event seems to be happening again and again.
* Repeated upsetting memories of the event.
* Nightly nightmares of traumatic events.
* Strong, uncomfortable reactions to situations that remind you of the event, people or places.

### 2. Avoidance

* Emotional "numbing," or feeling as though you don't care about anything.
* Feeling detached.
* Being unable to remember important aspects of the trauma.
* Having a lack of interest in normal activities.
* Showing less of your moods.
* Avoiding places, people, or thoughts that remind you of the event.
* Feeling like you have no future.

### 3. Arousal

* Difficulty concentrating, memory loss.
* Having an exaggerated response to things that startle you.
* Feeling more aware, safety conscious (hyper-vigilance).
* Feeling irritable or having outbursts of anger & rage.
* Having trouble falling or staying asleep.
* A lack of fear.

You might feel guilt about the event (including "survivor guilt").

You might also have some of the following symptoms, which are typical of anxiety, stress, and tension:

* Agitation or excitability
* Looping and intrusive thoughts
* Dizziness
* Fainting, losing consciousness
* Feeling your heart beat in your chest
* Headache
* Nausea & Dhiorrea
* Bed wetting
* Panic attacks
* Insomnia (not wanting to go to bed)

### Treatment

Treatment can help prevent PTSD from developing after a trauma. A good social support system may also help protect against PTSD.

If PTSD does occur, a form of treatment called "desensitization" may be used. This treatment helps reduce symptoms by encouraging you to go back to places where trauma occurred to deal with the emotions and feelings associated with the trauma. Over time, memories of the event should become less frightening.

### Expectations (prognosis)

You can increase the chance of a good outcome with:
Early diagnosis
Prompt treatment
Strong social support

### Common Complications

Alcohol abuse or other drug abuse
Depression
Panic attacks
Insomnia
Digestive disorders

### Seek help right away if:

* You feel overwhelmed.
* You are thinking of hurting yourself or anybody else.
* You are unable to control your behaviour.
* You have other very upsetting symptoms of PTSD.

# MUSIC THAT REPEATED OVER AND OVER STATE TO STATE ...

The Script - Breakeven

Journey - Don't Stop Believing

Rascal Flatts - Life Is A Highway

Sarah McLachlan - I Will Remember You

Christina Perri - Jar of hearts

Dolly Parton - Better Get to Livin'

Jason Aldean - Big Green Tractor

Luke Bryan - Rain Is A Good Thing

Wiz Kalifa - Black and Yellow

AC/DC - Thunderstruck

Men At Work - Down Under

Florence and the Machine - Dogs Days Are Over

# MUSIC THAT REPEATED OVER AND OVER STATE TO STATE ...

Lynyrd Skynyrd - Sweet Home Alabama

Jerrod Nieman - What Do You Want

Kings of Leon - Pyro

Katherine Jenkins - Hallelujah

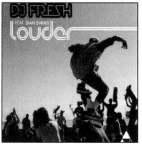

DJ Fresh - Louder

Kesha - Tik Tok

Pink – Glitter in the Air

Chris Brown - Beautiful People

Dizzee Rascal - Bonkers

The Charlie Daniels Band- The Devil Went Down to Georgia

Kenny Chesney - Who'd you be Today

Leona Lewis - Keep Bleeding

# MUSIC THAT REPEATED OVER AND OVER STATE TO STATE ...

Givers - Up, Up, Up

Lady Gaga - Poker Face

Katy Perry - California Gurls

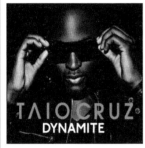

Taio Cruz - Dynamite

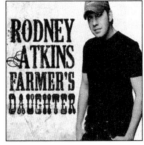

Rodney Atkins - Farmer's Daughter

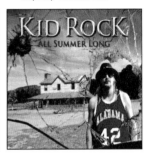

Kid Rock - All Summer Long

Jaron and the Long Road to Love– Pray For You

Aerosmith - Dream On

Pink - Raise Your Glass

The Fray - Over My Head

Depeche Mode - Just Can't Get Enough

Adele - Make You Feel My Love

19508608R00101

Made in the USA
Charleston, SC
28 May 2013